Obedience over Hustle

The Surrender of the Striving Heart

Malinda Fuller

SHILOH RUN  PRESS

An Imprint of Barbour Publishing, Inc.

Print ISBN 978-1-64352-075-9

eBook Editions:
Adobe Digital Edition (.epub) 978-1-64352-375-0
Kindle and MobiPocket Edition (.prc) 978-1-64352-376-7

Published by Shiloh Run Press, an imprint of Barbour Publishing, Inc., 1810 Barbour Drive, Uhrichsville, Ohio 44683, www.shilohrunpress.com

Our mission is to inspire the world with the life-changing message of the Bible.

Member of the
Evangelical Christian
Publishers Association

Printed in the United States of America.

Praise for *Obedience over Hustle*

"God always prizes obedience more than sacrifice! The fear of missing out has led many into unnecessary busyness—even tearing apart marriages and families in the pursuit of the elusive *more*. I'm thrilled for the release of *Obedience over Hustle* as Malinda helps alleviate the pressure to perform by reminding us that surrender triumphs over striving."

–John Bevere, bestselling author, minister,
co-founder of Messenger International

"Malinda is a lover of God who believes and stands for Truth. You will be encouraged, surprised, and blessed by her words."

–Havilah Cunnington, Bible teacher, international speaker, founder of Truth to Table ministry, and author of *Stronger than the Struggle*

"No matter how hard you hustle, your best efforts pale in comparison to what God can do through you. But before God can work through us, He has to work in us. And that's what *Obedience over Hustle* is all about: making the daily commitment to choose Him, and letting God direct your path, your pace, and your purpose. The truth in these pages reinforces the drastic difference between worldly pressure and God's peace."

–Michelle Myers, founder of She Works His Way

"In a world where we feel that we need to constantly go more and do more, Malinda's message of grace gives us a chance to breathe and free up our souls. You will feel lighter as you read her words of wisdom and follow God with more obedience rather than simply following the hustle mentality the world pushes us to!"

–Kara-Kae James, author of *Mom Up: Thriving with Grace in the Chaos of Motherhood* and executive director of Thrive Moms

"I have watched Malinda live out this message for years; she has faithfully and purposefully chosen obedience to Christ rather than the insistent demands of the world, and that choice has borne beautiful fruit—including the words you're holding in your hands. The good news in these pages is that obedience to Jesus is the sweetest gift to our souls—it's freedom rather than bondage and joy rather than despair. If you need a hope-filled reminder of why it's worth it to choose Jesus over everything else, this book is for you."

–Ann Swindell, author of *Still Waiting: Hope for When God Doesn't Give You What You Want*

"Read this. Read this. Read this. Malinda comes alongside you as a big sister, holds your hand, and shows you a better way. You'll find yourself nodding, underlining, and sending fist bumps high into the air as you read her words. She makes stories from the Bible come alive in a new and fresh way. You will finish *Obedience over Hustle* eager to listen to God's whispers of direction on your life and step into them."

—Rebecca Smith, founder of Better Life Bags and author of *A Better Life*

"Scripture is pretty clear about what Jesus followers are to do with his Good News. The problem is, the Gospel's implications are often counterintuitive to our flesh. Malinda does an excellent job of confronting culture with the language of heaven. Her words are gentle and complete in her invitation to choose God's abundance over the emptiness of what the world sells."

—Rach Kincaid, online coach and communicator

"The moment I heard the title of Malinda's new book, I just knew it would serve as a balm to my soul. *Obedience over Hustle* did just that. Full of scripture, grace, truth, and Malinda's wisdom, this book will take you into that holy space of saying yes to God's best and no to hustle. Buckle in for a gentle ride that will guide you toward a peaceful place of work, ministry, or whatever your calling. I'm personally a better woman because of Malinda's important book."

—Sarah Martin, speaker and author of *Just RISE UP!: A Call To Make Jesus Famous*

"Malinda Fuller twists the lens of your life into clarity of focus and gently asks, 'What do you see?' *Obedience over Hustle* will help you find the presence of Jesus in the small details of your busy life."

—Shelly Miller, author of *Rhythms of Rest, Finding the Spirit of Sabbath in a Busy World*

DEDICATION

*To my husband, Alex, for championing
my dreams as though they were his own*

CONTENTS

Closed Doors and Open Hands

I can still picture the hotel ballroom in Indianapolis. It was a Saturday night, the close of the conference, and scattered throughout the giant space, hundreds of women were joining in worship. Some stood at their circular tables with hands raised, others sat quietly, a few knelt on the floor. The lights had been dimmed, and from the small stage came the sounds of the husband-and-wife duo, him strumming softly on a guitar, her voice rising and falling like waves.

I was among the sitters—opting in this final session to be less expressive and remain silent. I closed my eyes, trying to connect with God. When I didn't hear the audible voice I was hoping for, I pulled my tattered journal from my purse and uncapped a pen. I quickly scrawled sentences across a page as tears dripped from the end of my nose, polka-dotting the crisp white backdrop with mascara stains. My hand jerked with the same intensity of my mind, which was screaming into the semidarkness.

I had already given God an ultimatum—as if that's ever a good idea. At the beginning of the conference, which I had flown across the country to attend, I had asked God to answer one prayer—just one. I wasn't expecting miraculous healing or writing on the wall. I wanted just a word (perhaps offered from a friend) or some glimmer of hope for the situation that I would fly back to California to face. Yet there I was, in the closing session of the event, and my *one* request remained unanswered.

What I'd demanded was a way out of the career I'd been working at for years. I loved helping people as a massage therapist, and the chiropractor I worked for was flexible and generous, but my heart wasn't truly in it anymore. Added to my three or four days at the office was the new role of "home educator" that I took on halfway through each weekday, as my family had just plunged into the world of homeschooling. My husband and I high-fived midday, trading off parenting duties, and on weekends he worked the bulk of his hours at his job, leaving me scrambling to find time for my growing passion—to become a writer and speaker. I had been burning the candle at both ends *and* in the middle.

My life at that time could best be described as one of "striving." I didn't want to keep my day job; I wanted to quit, but not bringing in any income wasn't even a consideration. My stable job kept us enjoying dinners out and date nights. It afforded plane tickets to see family for Christmas and the ability to get my hair done every other month. My husband's job provided for our regular expenses and kept us from racking up debt, but my income allowed breathing room in the budget for our family to have some fun. So for months I had been asking God for a new job, something that I could fit in around my family, like a part-time writing gig that I could do from home.

I wanted to "have it all," working part-time from my living room, homeschooling my children, and increasing my level of influence both online and in real life. I wanted God's provision, but I wanted it *my* way. I expected Him to fling a door wide open, but I didn't want any others to have to close first. And, of course, I wanted it in *my* timing, meaning I didn't want to have to do anything risky or brave.

The conference weekend in Indianapolis had been a Christmas gift from my husband—the chance to get away and build relationships within the network of creative Christian women I had been a part of. The event itself was designed to encourage and empower women to be influencers regardless of their budget, vocation, season of life, age, or location. It had been a great time of connecting with online friends over meals and in small group sessions, worshipping together, and hearing from amazing women. I'd had the opportunity to sit with an editor from a major publishing house who was full of encouraging words and support. And yet, in the final session before we all headed to our hotel rooms or rushed to the airport, I found myself disappointed. I had come into the weekend with anticipation that God was going to provide an easy solution to my problem—and He hadn't.

God's response to my pages full of angry journal inquiries was not at all what I had expected or hoped for. It didn't give me warm, fuzzy feelings, as I sometimes experience when I have a moment with God. It wasn't a beam of light or an audible voice, nor did anyone tap my shoulder and whisper a "word from the Lord" into my ear. It was one of those moments that leaves you stunned, and it was forever seared into my mind.

Nothing life-altering was happening in the room—no videos or teachers sharing a divine word, no crescendo of music from the stage. God's voice was quiet and unassuming, and no one else would have known that He was speaking directly to my heart. His response to my scathing thoughts was bold but gentle—firm but tender. He didn't chastise me for getting mouthy with Him as if I were a toddler throwing a fit on the floor. Instead, His posture was kind and simple; His words were whispered without the sting of guilt or shame. He didn't come at me in a rage, nor did He toss a passive-aggressive remark over His shoulder through a smirk. The question that was left suspended in the air between Him and me was simply, *"Will you obey Me?"*

My immediate response was, *Of course, Lord!* and then, with my eyes closed, I saw very clearly the image of a closed fist. It was a giant hand (like I would expect God's to look like) and it was white-knuckled and clenched tight.

I heard Him ask me, *"Am I not your provider?"* No booming voice jostled the lights above the table. It wasn't an audible question, but my heart started pounding just the same. I felt Him pressing on my chest, as if He was cocking an eyebrow and giving me the "Is that the truth?" look that I give my children when I know they aren't telling me the whole story.

Of course, God, You are my provider, is what my brain was programmed to respond and what I kept repeating over and over in my mind. And then I heard His third question: *"How can you say that I am when you hold so tightly to your job?"*

The singing continued around me as I sat thinking about these three questions: *"Will you obey Me?" "Am I not your provider?"* and *"How can you say that I am [your provider] when you hold so tightly to your job?"* I don't remember the song, how long it was sung, or how many minutes elapsed, but eventually my heart found a peaceful rhythm again. As I wrestled with those questions, I knew I had a choice to make—one decision that would change my family's bank account and calendar. And one that would require more faith than I had ever had to exert before.

I told God that night in Indiana, thousands of miles away from my family and home in California, that I trusted Him to be my provider. Even if it didn't make sense to quit my job without the safety net of an alternative income. Even if what I was about to do was like jumping from a plane without a parachute. Even if I felt foolish.

When I returned home the next day, I told my husband about the three questions and what I felt God was asking me to do. Without missing a beat, he responded, "Okay then, let's put a date on the calendar." And that's exactly what we did. In spite of great uncertainty regarding our finances and future, we decided to trust God and obey where He was asking us to risk. We were sure that God had a better way than what the world was screaming—the lie that said, "I can have everything, and be anything, if I just hustle a little harder."

— — —

Obedience over Hustle is organized into two sections: "Confronting the Hustle" and "Choosing Obedience." Chapter by chapter, we'll dig into biblical stories of radical obedience involving well-known and obscure characters alike. Also sprinkled throughout every chapter are real-life examples of contemporary women whose stories showcase courageous, immediate, and complete obedience; they have chosen to submit their dreams to God—despite how countercultural, challenging, or foolish it may appear—and pick up whatever task He has presented them with.

Closing out both sections is a summary with scripture references to dig into, key concepts to consider (as either personal or small group study), and journaling questions to help you dive deeper into the ideas presented in each chapter. You can flip to these pages as you move through the chapters, reflecting and answering questions as you read, or you can wait until the end of the section to go through the entire summary at once. Either way, I suggest you keep a journal or notebook nearby as you read so you can record your thoughts.

— — —

The affection that we have for hustle is not a modern one. Since Eden, individuals have manipulated God's plan and tried to fast-track His agenda in order to attain their dreams.

What we're after is honest reflection on where we have given in to the hustle and whether what it is producing is worth the effort. Is hustle fulfilling its promise of success and purpose, or have we become enslaved to it instead? The goal is not to persuade you to oppose a trend; instead, our aim should be to obey Jesus, regardless of what He's asking: Quit a job. Forgive a spouse. Give away some money. Live humbly. Risk big. Start small. Serve in obscurity. Build His kingdom.

By the final page, I hope you will eagerly and boldly say yes to whatever God asks and go wherever He leads, choosing obedience over hustle repeatedly, confidently, and passionately.

PART ONE

Confronting the Hustle

CHAPTER 1

This Thing Called Hustle

*H*ustle. It is impossible to ignore this idea.

Everyone has seen the word splashed across the front of a book jacket or coffee mug. It has made its mark on Instagram feeds. It isn't just a catchy phrase for the creatives camped out at the local brewhouse, nor is it reserved for business owners and those chasing down the next sale while sipping espresso. Moms of toddlers unite behind their gold-printed T-shirts proclaiming to the world that the "mommy hustle" is real. Christians are "prayin' and slayin'"—or eating, praying, and hustling, depending on the day.

When I first heard the word *hustle*, I was confused. I wondered why the bloggers I knew were using this term. I remember thinking, *What do you mean you're hustlin'?* It sounded bizarre. But then the hype took over and everyone started throwing the word around. All of a sudden, my social media feed brimmed with individuals pridefully announcing their "hustle" like they'd unlocked the secret code for doing super-cool things and achieving goals. They were the same women who'd always had the side business or creative hobby, the same writers, still working extra hard to be noticed, validated, and profitable. But now they had permission to race toward their goals—*hustle* wasn't just a verb; it had become a badge of honor to wear proudly. I know I used the word a few times, probably accented by a fist-bump emoji because, well, that's what you have to do to get people to notice your work. Or so I thought. It feels quite silly to admit that now.

In the months following the conference in Indiana, I found myself surrounded by the hustle noise. Everywhere I looked, I felt bombarded by the message that unless I was taking this Instagram class, I would never grow my social media platform; unless I was jumping on that writing retreat or conference, my dreams would never become a reality. Friends were taking advantage of opportunities for aspiring business owners, and the voice of hustle made all of it look so alluring.

As I started to see where I was giving in to the hustle, God poised more questions: *"If it's for My glory, why are you trying to do it your way, Malinda?" "If it doesn't happen in your time frame, will you be less effective, less happy, less fulfilled?" "What if My way looks different from how you see it—haven't My ways always been better?"*

Over a period of months, every book I picked up, every message I listened to, every article I read seemed to have the same undertones: the idea that if our hearts are striving after something other than God's goal for us, He won't bless our efforts. Even if we were to experience success through such means, it would come at a cost. This became a deafening conversation on repeat, and it was inescapable. Suddenly, the dialogue with my husband, my best friends, and random social media friends became, "What's up with the hustle?"

The more I heard and saw the hustle being promoted, the more curious I became: "Where did this notion come from?" I started to ask. "Why are we celebrating the back-breaking workaholism that it seems to advocate?" I decided to do some research.

The word *hustle* dates back to the mid-1600s to 1700s. The Dutch were the first to use it, and the translation meant "to shake."[1] I remember reading those first lines from the dictionary and thinking, *How did we get from "to shake" to the modern definition used to describe hard work?* Digging a little deeper, I unearthed a much longer list of definitions that provided insight into the word's evolution.

I noticed most of the historical uses of *hustle* were derogatory. It wasn't a title to bestow on your closest friend or loved one. *Hustler* was used to brand lowly characters, not to esteem hardworking individuals.

Listed below are some of the most common definitions I found for the word *hustle*:

- to push roughly
- to obtain by forceful action or persuasion
- to coerce or pressure someone into a choice
- to sell aggressively
- to swindle or cheat[2]

Of all the interpretations for this six-letter word, the modern version, "working hard, usually towards the common goal of creating an income,"[3] is the most widely used today, yet it is less commonly found in traditional dictionaries. The meaning of the word has morphed over the years from "to shake," to "to obtain by force," and eventually to "to put

---

[1] "Hustle Defined," Google Dictionary search result, https://www.google.com/search?q=hustle+defined&oq=hustle+defined&aqs=chrome..69i57j0l5.3752j0j7&sourceid=chrome&ie=UTF-8.

[2] Dictionary.com, s.v. "hustle," http://www.dictionary.com/browse/hustle?s=t.

[3] Urban Dictionary, s.v. "HUSTLE (2)," last modified May 14, 2015, http://www.urbandictionary.com/define.php?term=Hustle.

a lot of effort into one's work." Interestingly, this last definition isn't the same "hustle" message that our grandparents and great-grandparents knew. Those who lived through the war eras knew that *hustle* meant to provide for one's family, but today the connotation is much more explicit.

— — —

- *Hustle invigorates me and fuels my fire to "GO."*
- *Fortune favors the brave.*
- *Use as much energy as you can to get to the finish.*
- *Work hard to hit a goal. [Hustle] makes me feel excited for what's to come.*
- *Hustle equals drive. Those who hustle are entrepreneurs. They are "doers" and get stuff done. They are like Nehemiah. . .who saw and filled the need.*
- *[Hustle is] giving everything I have into one concentrated thing.*

These were some of the responses I received when I asked my Facebook community, "What feelings does the word 'hustle' stir up?"

If you just read these thoughts and felt your heart beating wildly in excitement, then you're probably one of those who picked up this book because of your love for the hustle. You send out virtual fist bumps to your friends who are growing their sales teams and crushing goals in their businesses, and you wake up eager to tackle your to-dos for the day and check off items from your goals list. This six-letter word gets your blood pumping. Each time you say it, your adrenaline surges like a wave cresting just off the beach. More than likely you are a creative, an entrepreneur, a builder of things or teams or people. Perhaps you love sales and networking, or maybe you're a dreamer with a five-year plan that you keep posted on your bathroom mirror. You are a three, eight, or one on the Enneagram personality model, and you enjoy setting audacious goals and then surprising everyone when you crush them early.

If you're a Christian and a lover of the hustle, then you probably know where to find verses that sound like this: "I worked hard at building the wall of Jerusalem. All my men gathered there to work on the wall."[4] These lines from the book of Nehemiah are like balm to your soul when you find yourself being told to "slow down" by friends and family. They're the permission you need to continue pushing forward at the breakneck speed you've been racing. As a planner and overachiever, you tend to be hypercritical of yourself and typically see your efforts as never quite good enough—which just pushes you even harder. You always have a "word for the year," live by your day planner, and struggle to embrace the idea of "rest."

Even if you're not in the business world, this hustle hunger has bled over into other aspects of your life. You demand perfection from others—your spouse, family members, friends, children, and coworkers. You probably expect everyone to have the same drive and passion as you and become easily frustrated when others have no ambition to set goals for their personal development. If you see yourself in these characterizations, rest assured, you're in good company. In fact, these descriptors are fairly accurate of my

---

[4] Nehemiah 5:16 ERV

own personality and tendencies. You are *not* weird, crazy, or alone if you are wired this way.

This book was not written to guilt or to shame you. Its pages are not meant to overwhelm or condemn but to offer freedom—a pass to jump into the deep end of the pool called grace. The message here is not that working hard, having goals, and even being wildly successful are bad things. I want to make one thing very clear: I am not against small businesses, women pursuing their dreams, or mothers who work from home—I am one of those hard-working women myself. I applaud those who are chasing after their dreams—if those dreams are God-given and, even more important, God-authorized. (In chapter 17 we'll discuss the idea that sometimes our goals are from God but He hasn't approved the timing.)

Rather than condemning those with lofty ambitions, those defying the odds with their achievements, I'm suggesting that our lives have become overrun by an incessant striving for something more. The hustling heart reaches its fingers deep, infiltrating far beyond just our livelihood. Its chant chokes out the conversation of contentment and gratitude until our "wants" masquerade as "needs." I'm not here to advocate slothful behavior and apathetic living; I'm here with one question: Is what you're hustling after the thing that God has asked you to do?

In our me-centered world where we believe we can become anything we set our minds to and attain anything we feel we deserve, it is no longer enough to just put a lot of effort into our work—we have to hustle after it. "It" being the variable. For some, hustling after "it" means earning a paycheck or achieving a goal. Others are seeking to attain more of something: clients, power, success, influence, fame.

"A lot of effort" simply isn't enough anymore. We're expected to be competitive, focused, and driven—every day, all day. We aren't happy to just "work smarter"; we have to be both smart and relentless in the pursuit of our goals. We need to complete our work faster, and with better results, than everyone else. It's as though our entire lives are a giant game of Monopoly where we're creating side deals and one-upping everyone in our circle, continually positioning ourselves for recognition, validation, and success.

For some of you reading, maybe the hustle looks more like "keeping up" with those in your neighborhood, at the gym, online, or at church. Maybe you've experienced the suffocating feeling of the need to prepare all-organic homemade meals, return to your prepregnancy weight at six weeks postpartum, keep your home sparkling clean (despite having two toddlers at home), read ten books a month, and slay your business goals a week before the end of each month. Does this sound familiar?

For new college graduates, the hustle might look like chasing after a dream job that can help you pay back your mountain of debt. But rather than working hard toward that goal, you may find yourself in the perennial trap of the hustle: bouncing from one position to the next trying to find the "right environment," struggling to commit to the nine-to-five, eating and drinking your paycheck away, and splurging on impressive items and trips. Because that's what you're supposed to do—according to social media.

To those who have graduated kids and now find themselves in the next season of life, the hustle song sounds different yet. You may not care in the slightest about posting on Instagram, chasing sales, or climbing a ladder of success, but that doesn't mean your heart doesn't strive. Maybe it's for your ministry, book, church, or business to do well. Maybe it's to keep up with your friend's house, car, body, or luxury vacations. You may not be someone who struggles with listening to God when it comes to writing a check, but you know He's been telling you for years to befriend a neighbor, foster some children, mentor a young businesswoman, host a foreign exchange student, start a Bible study, or lead a women's group at church—and you've continued to find other things to do so that you're "too busy" to follow through on what He's asking.

The hustle looks a little different for each of us, but its nature of striving is always the same. Hustling is chasing after a goal at any cost. It's the pushing that comes from a heart focused on what others have and what others are doing, rather than choosing contentment and listening for the voice of God. We've traded hearing God's simple "Well done" in our current season (our current budget, our current circumstance) for gaining the applause of the masses.

— — —

The hustling heart drives us—from making sure our skin, travel schedules, and homes measure up to the social media noise. We tally how successful our side business is right out of the gate, strive to calculate the reach of our influence, and work to prove the worthiness of our cause—right alongside our closest friends and allies. We question God's timing, His ways, His failure to move on our behalf, even while at the same time crying out, "Your way, Lord!"

What is this obsession with a word once rarely used—

hustle? Why have we elevated this concept, carrying it around like a banner, chanting it for everyone to hear? Are we seeking validation for our achievements or our efforts? Who is our audience—and to what end are we performing? These are just a few of the questions we're going to tackle over the next several chapters. Are you ready? Let's go!

CHAPTER 2

Suffocating under the Hustle

*I'm pretty sure in the Garden of Eden the serpent had
"hustle" on his deceptive lips. If Eve had [decided] to
be still and reflect and pause over the moment, perhaps
she may have chosen differently. Hustle creates a false
urgency to act and move based on deception of who
we are and what we need, yet hustle is seen as a "good
thing" in our culture of women. If we don't hustle,
then we won't get what is ours or what we "deserve."
So we are told to hustle and move quick. . .and then
feel guilty when we rest or aren't pushing ourselves.
It's a crazy thing, that thing called hustle.*

When I began to share with friends and other writers
about how the hustle had affected me on a personal level,
I was surprised by their responses. The general feeling
was that of suffocation. I had no idea how many people
had been experiencing similar angst over this word. The
epigraph above is from an online friend who responded
to my questions about how the word made her feel.
Crowdsourcing brought forth emotional responses from
people who were burnt out and looking to mend what
they had inadvertently broken as a result of their hustling. Some answers were simple, others strong—some
even combative. As I did more research and probed
further, I discovered that the stress of the hustle is a

widespread concern. Here's a sampling of the comments I received regarding the implications of the word *hustle*:

> *It has very negative connotations to me. I see it used constantly, and it's often with people/brands that are prioritizing their business goals above all else; [who] see working fifty-five-hour weeks as a sign of being passionate and earning their success.*

> *[When I hear the word hustle] I feel stressed immediately.*

> *It gives me heart palpitations.*

> *For me, it's a dangerous word. It tempts me to sin and fool myself into thinking I can function out of my own strength.*

From all over the country and across oceans, individuals were joining the conversation. They were skeptical of the message that there is only one way to become successful (and questioning the markers used to measure "success"), and they were tired of feeling compelled to claw themselves into the spotlight, following the advice of "industry leaders," and grow a big platform. Outside of the creative circles I was involved in, I heard mothers respond to the idea of "trying to do it all," and shop owners admit that despite all they'd poured into their businesses, they were choosing to shut them down because they had become something that God didn't want them to focus on anymore. The idea of "success" was confusing to women who were stay-at-home mothers intent on loving their families well, yet drowning beneath the message "God has more for you than *just* being a mom."

As the hustle noise continued to grow louder all around me, so did God's whisper to my heart: *"Is that what I've called you to?"* Just as it had in the hotel ballroom, His voice came softly, gently, with grace. As I pondered whether the chase was worth it, other messages surfaced: *"Stay humble. Be still. Rest. Build people, not things. Trust Me. Seek first My kingdom, not your empire."*

That last one was a zinger, not because I had any lofty goals—my aim wasn't to reach superstar status as a writer—but because I did feel that God had gifted me with the ability to string together words, and I wanted the opportunity to share them. I wasn't seeking a six-figure income, but my heart did want a sphere of influence. I wanted to teach the Bible to women and share messages of hope and truth with crowds. It didn't seem like a selfish goal, but eventually I realized I also longed for the affirmation those opportunities provided.

If you are nodding, waving your white flag, or crying in your chair, then the very thought of the hustle probably causes your palms to sweat and your mouth to go dry. You read or hear the word and instantly cringe, curling inward like a turtle retreating into its shell when threatened. *Hustle* brings weighty pressure—to perform and please, to hurry and overwork, to strive after recognition or power; the feelings it evokes are oppressive to you. You tend to shy away from competition and comparison because you realize those things rob you of your joy. You recognize that not all goals justify the cost necessary to achieve them and often wonder if those around you will ever come to the same conclusion.

You see the hard work of others as slavery or perhaps as just outright ridiculous: *Why would anyone want to work that hard?!* is something you are often left wondering. Perhaps you've never been one to set goals, and you don't understand when others describe doing so as a "need." Regardless of your Enneagram number or Meyer-Briggs result, your definition of work ethic looks vastly different from theirs. They say, "Hustle!" and you roll your eyes and think, *Workaholic.* The verse you take refuge in comes straight from the mouth of Solomon, who uttered, "Throughout their life, they have pain, frustrations, and hard work. Even at night, a person's mind does not rest. This is also senseless."[5]

Senseless—that's exactly how you perceive this whole hustle commotion. And it's that idea that drew you to the message of obedience over hustle.

— — —

The idea of personal branding has become common in our culture. Moms hand out cards for their home-based businesses just as quickly as dads who hold nine-to-five sales jobs. Creatives, communicators, and entrepreneurs alike are turning to social media to build a platform and expand their influence. Facebook, Instagram, Twitter, and Pinterest are no longer applications for "the younger generation"; rather, the chant is that everyone needs to be connected to everyone else—*all the time.*

One of my favorite Bible teachers, author Beth Moore, has addressed this idea of personal branding with refreshing truth and boldness on her blog. Of the many lines that

---

[5] Ecclesiastes 2:23 ERV

I wanted to underline on my screen (and then shout from the rooftops) was the challenge to online influencers to stop confusing the building of their own following with the building of the church. Her encouragement was to stop selling ourselves in the name of Jesus—even if that is the popular advice shared by experts and modeled by leaders. Her passionate words left me feeling convicted but not judged; they were yet another echo of the message that had been on repeat: *"Focus on what I've asked you to do, Malinda; stop the striving and obey."*

I knew I'd been guilty of doing the exact thing she was warning against. I'd given in to the idea that to be influential, I had to be big—and so I'd hustled harder. I "needed" ten thousand followers before I could even think about publishing a book, because the experts say it's your loyal tribe that will promote your work. So rather than sharpening my skills as a writer, I invested in trying to understand and become successful in the social media world. Instead of caring about the quality of my words, I fixated on quantity. I had been consumed with what others were saying instead of what God was saying about me. I spent time and money growing followers and lists because that was most important—*except it really wasn't.*

God had not asked me to build a giant social media platform. He didn't need me to have 150,000 social media followers. He had asked me to focus my time on other things, none of which included spending hours "networking" with strangers over the phone or throwing money at classes meant to increase my impact on Instagram. He had asked me to focus on nurturing real-life relationships and honing my gift. Neither of those assignments was very glamorous, just as being a stay-at-home mother, home educator, good neighbor, or faithful follower of Jesus may earn the applause of Jesus but seldom anyone else.

To be honest, I'd once been a fond member of the hustle crowd. I shook my fist alongside friends who were intent on being noticed and admired. I sold my authenticity and contentment in order to expand my reach. Sadly, I've watched many friends get swallowed up by the belief that the cost of "doing it all" is worth it.

I have spent years now fighting against the powerful seduction to gain influence and acclaim by any means. Unfortunately, my efforts didn't quench the hunger of my heart for significance, nor silence the hustle chant. The noise is louder than ever. Contentment is not what we are fighting for as much as "quiet"—just a simple reprieve from the din that surrounds us, taunting us with the notion that our value is somehow connected to how many people follow us, how productive we are in a day, and what other people are saying about us.

Chances are what God has called you to isn't shiny, sexy, or lucrative. More than likely it is ripe with anonymous moments and mundane tasks. He doesn't ask everyone to write Grammy-nominated worship songs, plant a church, or start the next nonprofit that millennials everywhere will sleep in their cars to work at. God doesn't expect us all to be like Noah, Joseph, David, or the apostle Paul. But He does call all of us into a life defined by obedience.

My goal is not to persuade you to oppose a message but, instead, to encourage you to obey Jesus. To choose to listen to His voice, follow where He's leading, and yield where He's asking you to lay down your will, idea, timelines, or dream. To choose obedience both in the tiniest of details and in the grandest of plans. To walk away from the clawing for attention and the seeking after validation, and to be satisfied with what God has already said about you. "Obedience over hustle" is not just a phrase to replace the chant of "hustle harder" with another equally trendy slogan. It's more than a belief, more than something you can tweet, pin, or print for the inspiration board hanging over your desk. Saying no to the suffocating chant of hustle and yes to obedience is a daily decision, a way of thinking—a lifestyle.

CHAPTER 3

But Didn't God Institute Hard Work?

"Adam, dinner is ready!"

From his crouched position on the ground, he heard his wife calling. He watched Eve's slow movements and smiled at the sight of her protruding belly. It seemed that her skin seemed to stretch more each day, and the jabbing pains she felt from the inside were increasing in their intensity also. The heat of the day coupled with her chores quickly exhausted his wife these days.

Adam jumped up and gathered the food he'd just pulled from the earth. He piled the vegetables into Eve's open arms and rubbed the small of her back with a hand that was calloused and dirty. He glanced down and noted how he had aged in recent years. The skin on his face, arms, and back had been baked by the sun; the soles of his feet had grown thick—a better defense against the thorns and rocks he battled daily.

Adam smiled at the food set before him, and with eyes pointed toward the heavens and Eve's hand in his, he offered thanks to God. For the food before them, the strength to tend to his work and care for his wife, and the rain that had come to quench the earth just yesterday, making the ground more forgiving during today's harvest.

Later that night Adam watched as his wife

*brought forth the fruit of their union. Her body
surged under the pains that seemed to come violently
with little reprieve. He had seen animals give birth
to countless offspring, but to watch his wife writhe
with pain was something else altogether. Eve clung
to Adam as she bore down, and gripping him tightly,
she pushed her firstborn into the world. Minutes later
Adam watched as Eve finally lay back. Completely
drained, drenched with sweat, and with tears running down her cheeks, she nestled the babies against
her chest.*

*Adam met her eyes and together, just as they had
done earlier that evening, they offered up thanks to God.
For the strength of their bodies that came from their
Maker—the ability to carry out the tasks they were
designed to bear, not without pain, or blood, or tears,
but with grace nonetheless.*

*C*hristians, I've learned, are some of the first to jump on
the hustle train and use the word interchangeably with *hard
work*. Tucked into their journals or taped to their bathroom mirrors are Bible verses about working hard and
God's blessing. After all, God honors those who rise early
and create a plan, doesn't He? Perhaps you've read the
account of creation in Genesis and felt justified in your
work because God Himself—the Creator—worked so
hard that He then took a day to rest. (As a side note, I'm
not sure God "needed" a day to rest as much as we "needed"
an example of how to live our lives, but I digress.) Who
am I to tell you that hustle is offensive when successful

Christian women and leaders are telling you to pull yourself up by your bootstraps and "get after it"?

I get it. The truth is, I'm not against working hard. Nor am I advocating the belief that because God is our Provider, we shouldn't be diligent, or that if we pray hard enough, He will grant us health, wealth, and prosperity. Rather, I believe that the hard work God wants us to do is in partnership with Him, rather than just us working hard to achieve personal goals or asking Him to bless whatever we put our hand to as if He's a genie who moves at our every request.

Starting in Genesis, with Adam and Eve tending the garden, all the way through to the end of the New Testament, we see examples of the way life is given meaning when we work in conjunction with God toward His purposes. Hundreds of scripture verses point us back to the idea that God honors us when we work hard. Of all the books of the Bible, the lines of Proverbs abound in work-ethic wisdom:

A son who works hard while it is harvest time will be successful, but one who sleeps through the harvest is worthless.[6]

Riches come to those who work hard.[7]

Those who work hard get plenty.[8]

If you work hard, you will have plenty.[9]

---

[6] Proverbs 10:5 ERV

[7] Proverbs 12:27 ERV

[8] Proverbs 13:4 ERV

[9] Proverbs 14:23 ERV

There is no denying it—God desires that we work hard. Paul says in 2 Thessalonians, "We never accepted food from anyone without paying for it. We worked hard day and night so we would not be a burden to any of you."[10] Paul was not talking about his ministry of preaching and teaching. He and other missionaries maintained a business that would support them financially so that they wouldn't have to rely on the church to meet their needs.[11] This is a good reminder for Christians to be diligent workers and not lay unnecessary financial burdens on others, yet I don't think that Paul's tentmaking business would fall into the esteemed category of a "side hustle" today. The difference in Paul's work/life situation was that his day job didn't interfere with what he felt called by God to do—to take the Good News to the Gentiles. Even though he had a job, it never caused him to lose sight of those things of eternal impact.

Before we go any further, I want to define a few more terms because of all the feedback I received on the topic of hustle. The words *hard work* and *workaholism* appeared most frequently. To start, let's look at the phrase *work ethic*: "a belief in the moral benefit and importance of work and its inheritability to strengthen character."[12]

Next, let's define the term *workaholic*: "a person who works compulsively at the expense of other pursuits."[13]

The dictionary states that work ethic strengthens one's character. This definition oozes with integrity and honor —a stark contrast to the list of words used to describe a

---

[10] 2 Thessalonians 3:8 NLT

[11] Acts 18:2–3

[12] Dictionary.com, s.v. "work ethic (n.)," http://www.dictionary.com/browse/work-ethic?s=t.

[13] Dictionary.com, s.v. "workaholic (n.)," http://www.dictionary.com/browse/workaholic?s=t.

hustler. One understanding bolsters hustling as an activity worth pursuing—a hustler as a person worth holding in high esteem. The other is like a heavy shackle around the neck, seeing hustling as compulsive work *at the expense of other pursuits.*

What would happen if we exchanged the words *other pursuits* in the definition of *workaholic* with *relationships, health, peace of mind,* or *contentedness?* How would we feel using *hustle* if it was defined this way? We cross the threshold between working hard and being a workaholic when the need to work comes at the expense of other things.

There's no denying it: God honors a good work ethic. Not our minimal efforts or apathetic attitudes, but our *hard work.* The physical act of toiling for a day's meal was His idea. In Genesis 3, after Adam and Eve confess their sin, God hands out consequences, and to Adam He says, "By the sweat of your brow will you have food to eat until you return to the ground."[14]

While Adam received punishment for his sin, the actual curse fell not on him but on the ground. Rather than curse the first man (and all his offspring to come), God turned to the earth He created and positioned it against Adam forever: "The ground is cursed because of you. All your life you will struggle to scratch a living from it. It will grow thorns and thistles for you, though you will eat of its grains."[15]

I can only imagine the ground crying out against what seems like an unjust sentence. And yet I have to believe that God chose this consequence out of His incredible

---

[14] Genesis 3:19 NLT

[15] Genesis 3:17–18 NLT

mercy and abundant love for the pinnacle of His creation: humankind. While He could have gathered together the angels and told them, *"Well, sorry about all the excitement, but we're going to have to start over,"* He didn't. Instead, He cursed the ground, causing what was fruitless (thistles and thorns) to spring up and make tending the land a difficult task for Adam. God said, "You will work hard for your food, until your face is covered with sweat."[16]

Just to clarify, Adam's purpose was always to work with God in the garden. In the very beginning of Genesis, we read that God "put the man in the Garden of Eden to work the soil and take care of the garden."[17] God's intention was that Adam would know what a "solid day's work" looked like. Adam was cared for, but he also had to work in conjunction with what God had provided; the land needed to be tended. And we all know that when we work hard for things, we tend to appreciate them more. (I can only imagine how delicious his harvest must have been!) What's interesting is that when God gave instructions to Adam to "work" the soil, He didn't use the word *labor*, *toil*, or *strive*. None of these words appeared until after the Fall.

I want to highlight two specific words that tend to get lost. After Adam and Eve ate the forbidden fruit, God spelled out that Adam was *now* going to have to work by the sweat of his brow[18] (considerably more effort than what was previously required) just to feed his family. The three syllables I'm going to camp on for just a moment are "a living." These two words are what Adam would

---

[16] Genesis 3:19 ERV

[17] Genesis 2:15 ERV

[18] Genesis 3:19 NLT

struggle with for the rest of his life: to scratch a living from the ground.

What was the point of Adam's sweat? To scratch a living.

A living.

Not to acquire wealth.

Not to amass an inconceivable fortune.

Not to make a great name for himself.

Nope. None of those things.

The point was just to make a living (or *livelihood*): to support his existence.[19]

The fact that God made it harder for Adam to feed his family is fascinating, because what had Adam been doing until then? Adam and Eve had been eating the bounty of the garden. They hadn't been starving because up until that moment, the ground had been flourishing on its own.

It sprouted food at the whisper of God's voice. He spoke, and the earth bore fruit. The Bible says that God planted the garden and made the vegetation grow and the rivers flow.[20] But after the Fall, it was up to Adam to work for his meals. He would have to sweat. The most beautiful revelation of this dark chapter in Genesis is that God didn't wipe His hands of Adam and Eve; He didn't abandon them in their hour of need. Even though Adam would now have to work hard, and by the sweat of his brow scratch a living, he was still working *with* God (and God always planned to do the heavy lifting). Adam was successful in his job only when he worked in tandem with God.

How many farmers do you know who can take full

---

[19] Dictionary.com, s.v. "livelihood (n.)," http://www.dictionary.com/browse/livelihood.

[20] Genesis 2:8–10

credit for the crops they harvest? Isn't it God who provides the rain that falls and sends worms and animals to fertilize the earth? Isn't it the Creator of the sun who tells it when to rise and when to stay hidden, who commands the winds to blow in the seasons? Isn't it God who whispers photosynthesis into existence and turns a single seed into a seed-bearing plant? The farmer doesn't lend a hand to any of those processes. The farmer merely tends the crops—protecting, maintaining, and stewarding the ground, but never actually producing anything through some personal power.

Perhaps the strong work ethic that God desired for Adam was less about what Adam could do for himself and more about where Adam's reliance lay. Maybe God wanted to introduce an environment where Adam would have to partner with Him in order to produce what he needed to live. Adam learned how to work hard, but he also learned how to depend on God—how to pray for rain and sunshine and favorable outcomes. I believe this dependence is the difference between hard work and hustle.

The hustling heart is all about what "I" can do. I come up with "my" goals and push myself to achieve them. Hustlers are intent on creating something fabulous using their own power, operating on their own schedule, and working to advance their own name. But God desires that our partnership with Him would make *His* name great—that our most significant accomplishments would not make us rich and famous (or powerful and influential) but rather point people to Jesus.

At the end of the day, aware of having played only a part in the sowing and reaping process, the farmer gives thanks *to God* for the bounty on the table, without whom nothing could be produced. In the same way, we too must admit that our greatest efforts, without the hand of God working in tandem, produce a crop that is left wanting.

God will hold us accountable for what He has given us to steward just as He does with the farmer. The harvest that feeds others is the result of the faithful tending of the farmer. But it is only in partnership with God that the remarkable happens.

And our lifework is no different.

CHAPTER 4

The Better Thing

"Wipe the sweat before it drips off your face, Martha! Knead that bread faster! Jesus and the disciples have been traveling a long way, and they're probably famished; you'd better move it! You don't want to keep the Master waiting, do you?" The inner dialogue is on repeat as she moves quickly from one task to the next. She smiles briefly, happy with her progress as well as her ability to multitask so well.

Chanting, stirring, sweating, murmuring, and sighing, Martha moves toward the cooking fire to turn the meat. She keeps a watchful eye on the door with a silent prayer that her sister, Mary, will miraculously appear and offer help. As the minutes tick by, Martha's inner dialogue shifts: "Where is that sister of mine, anyway? Surely she remembers that it's our role as women to serve our guests! Especially when one of those guests is Jesus!" She's fuming; her blood pressure is almost as elevated as the fire's temperature. "I can't believe she's so thoughtless!" she mutters under her breath. "What is so important that she can't be bothered to come and help me?"

One of the most passionate responses I received during the crowdsourcing portion of my research came from a Christian woman who was *all* for hustle. She is a dreamer and a doer, eager to join the hustle chant. She said that Christians need to get off their "donkeys" and get to work. She sided with Martha, who was a go-getter and an over-achiever, and said that we should "admire Martha for her hustle (service) just as we do Mary, who sat still in her worship."

Part of me wholeheartedly agreed with this gal. I had observed many Christians with a less-than-stellar work ethic, offering minimal effort and then expecting (or demanding) God to show up in His power and make up for their lack. To be fair, I've probably identified more with Martha over the years than with Mary, as I am also a doer. Like her, I have been a complainer and martyr, because that's the posture we tend to take when we realize we are working hard and others are sitting. I can easily defend this woman's cause—that we should admire Martha for her service. Chances are, Martha took great pride in her work. Hence the need to point out to Jesus all that she had been slaving over. Poor girl; she just wanted some validation!

Boy, does that ever sound familiar.

What do you think Jesus' response would have been if Martha had quietly continued to go about her work? If she had brought in the meal and set it at Jesus' feet without the emotional outburst, would her offering have been more acceptable? I have to think so. I don't believe Jesus was as concerned with what Martha was doing in the next room as He was interested in what was happening inside her heart.

We tend to forget that the things we are passionate about, naturally gifted at, and interested in do not come as a surprise to God. He gave us the personalities and dreams we have; He is purposeful in the way He creates each of us. The Bible doesn't say what Martha went on to do after Jesus returned to heaven, but I imagine she was always busy. Why? Because that's how God wired her; it was part of His design for her. He made her a doer, a hostess—someone with a passion for cooking, opening her home, and serving people.

I believe Martha came alive when she was meeting the needs of others, and this fact didn't go unnoticed by Jesus. He would have been fully aware of Martha's busyness in the kitchen even without seeing the sweat beaded on her forehead or her flushed cheeks as she stood over the fire. Jesus could see inside of her. He understood the rush she felt when operating in her gifts. Hospitality came naturally to Martha—it was what she loved—and part of God's heart was bursting with pride as He watched her bustling about.

Jesus' condemnation wasn't in regard to Martha's dinner preparations, her work ethic, or her personality. He was peering into her heart when He spoke the words, "You are concerned with many things." I imagine the tenderness in His voice. He didn't want to embarrass or shame her. Jesus knew Martha; He was the One who knit her together in her mother's womb. He formed her heart and knew her need for recognition. With smiling eyes, He continued, ". . .but few are needed."

Maybe you've heard a similar whisper: *"You are doing too many things. . . . You are striving and multitasking and chasing productivity. . . . You are eager to serve, but out of what motive?"*

This is exactly what I felt God whispering to my heart

at that conference in Indiana. *"Malinda, you're doing too many things."* I knew it was the truth. I was juggling too much and not doing any of it well. I was exhausted from striving over what was in front of me, all the while comparing what I was doing to what others were not *and* getting mad at Jesus in the process.

I love this story of Martha and Mary—the one we've heard referenced at every women's event regardless of the theme, speaker, or time of year:

> *But Martha was distracted by all the preparations that had to be made. She came to [Jesus] and asked, "Lord, don't you care that my sister has left me to do the work by myself? Tell her to help me!"*
>
> *"Martha, Martha," the Lord answered, "you are worried and upset about many things, but few things are needed—or indeed only one. Mary has chosen what is better."*[21]

There's a reason Joanna Weaver's book *Having a Mary Heart in a Martha World* is a bestseller and why so much of the conversation in modern Christian women's circles is about "abiding" with Jesus. The idea isn't new. Creating time to intentionally *be* with Jesus, as opposed to *doing* things for Him or in His name, is what women have struggled with since the beginning of time. This story from Luke 10 is well known, and most of us can easily identify with one sister more than the other. We also know the one we need to emulate more.

---

[21] Luke 10:40–42 NIV

I love the grace that Jesus extended to Martha in their exchange. Rather than chastise her, He gave her a thought to ponder—six words that couldn't be ignored. He said, "Mary has chosen the better thing."[22] He didn't offer a three-point sermon on what exactly Mary was doing, and He certainly didn't say, "Why can't you be more like your sister?"

Jesus' carefully chosen words remind us that often we will have to decide between the good and the better thing.

My friend Tabitha recently found herself at this type of intersection. She is a young mother with an enormous heart for God and people and giant dreams of how He might use her gift of communication to influence and impact lives. She is a fellow writer and speaker with a fabulous creative streak. She's always trying new things, saying yes to opportunities that scare her, and planning how she can better share her message with women. But her decisions haven't always been easy.

Tabitha's test of obedience came right on the heels of baby number two. Of course, baby number two was right on the heels of the first, leaving her with a full-time career and two children under two. With a master's degree to pay off and a fulfilling career as a school counselor, it only made sense for her to go back to work. She wasn't just returning to a job after her maternity leave was over—she was resuming something she loved, something she was good at, something that gave her a rich sense of purpose. She was also adamant about *not* becoming a stay-at-home mother—one of the first things she'd told her husband

22 Luke 10:42 NCV

after they were married. But the whispers came, urging her to hang up her professional career for a season in order to be fully present while at home raising her babies.

Over the years, I have lost track of the number of times we have encouraged each other with the words, "What's God called you to *now*?" We are constantly helping each other determine whether the goal or dream or project we are pursuing is something that God wants us to work hard toward in our current season of life.

Tabitha's dream of writing a book and teaching women still burns brightly. Does she continue to struggle with wanting more from her life than changing diapers and cleaning up after (now) energetic toddlers? Absolutely! Have there been moments when she questioned whether she made the right decision? She has admitted so. But at the end of the day, would she change her decision? Not a chance. Why?

Tabitha knows the voice of the One who spoke her dreams into being. She has learned to heed those promptings when they come. She knows that just as God asked her to step out of her career for a season, He will again give her peace to step back into it if and when the time is right. And instead of becoming bitter about the mundaneness of her days, she's choosing to be the influential leader God has created her to be, right now.

Even though she doesn't have a giant platform, she is using her unapologetic voice to bring healing and inspiration to others through social media, podcasting, and speaking events. She has gathered together women from all seasons and denominations in her city for mornings of Bible conversation and food. She meets together with other moms to encourage and strengthen them on a regular basis; and most importantly, she has sunk deep into the trenches of motherhood with an eternal perspective. Rather than dread and wish away these years of early development, she is going after the hearts of her children, intent on raising them to love and follow Jesus.

Tabitha heard the taunting of the world that to be influential, for her life to have purpose, she had to be big and loud. But instead of chasing what other people are doing, she has plugged herself into her family and her community, because that's what obedience looks like for her in this season. Laying down the hustle meant being content with being small. It meant owning the role of mother without coveting what others can do. She has said yes to God, given up the hustle, and stepped into obedient living.

I believe this is where many of us find ourselves: We are busy, like Martha, pursuing "many things." We're juggling children and work, husbands and health; we're volunteering at church and charities we care deeply for; and we're carving out time for our hobbies and creative pursuits. We make room for friendships and travel, classes and cooking, and the list goes on and on. All of these things can be good, especially if God has given us a passion for them, but they can't all be "the better thing."

It's impossible to dismiss Jesus' tender yet not-so-subtle message: "You're missing it, Martha. You're doing too much; your priorities are messed up, and you need to refocus." This message is what more and more people are tuning in to. It's like they're waking up from a dream only to realize that they're missing the more important things. They have been hustling and sacrificing, striving and clawing their way toward a goal only to get there and ask, "Was it worth it?"

Here's a clue: if the hustle is causing strife in your relationships, the answer to the above question is probably no. God isn't going to ask you to sacrifice healthy relationships to pursue His purpose for your life. That's not His nature.

Some of you may be reading this with tears streaming down your face because you know you've been doing the Martha dance. You've been busying yourself with all sorts of things, hustling hard for validation and seeking approval from anyone and everyone who will give it generously. You've found yourself growing bitter, and you've gone to God (like Martha) pointing fingers in the direction of other people, reminding Him how hard you've been working. Maybe your hustle has even been "in His name," and you want to feel justified, but instead the feeling growing in your heart is that perhaps your priorities need to shift.

Friend, know that you're in good company. For me, this struggle—to keep what is most important as my daily priority—is an ongoing one. I don't think this single encounter with Jesus was enough to change Martha's heart forever. Maybe it was, but I doubt it. It was probably an echo that she heard for the rest of her life.

Maybe you're not burning the candle at both ends at work, but you are wearing yourself out trying to keep up with the expectations and demands of others. With countless books lining the shelves and articles flooding our inboxes with ways to "be more productive," "achieve results in less time," and "live the life you want to live," it's normal to feel overwhelmed. Perhaps this reminder from scripture can serve as your pass to pull back, do less, and refocus on the things that matter most. Instead of chasing after "could-bes" in the future, choose to dive deep into what's in front of you now: the people and opportunities of the present—the *better* things.

Chapter 5

Artificial Significance

She shuffles from the coffee bar toward me without looking up from her phone. Without a sound, she slumps into the stiff white plastic chair across the table from me and drops her purse to the floor. Her makeup is flawless, her hair pulled back into a perfectly messy bun high on top of her head, yet her eyes look heavy. Not in a sleepy way, justifying the triple-shot espresso she just ordered. She looks tired in a mental way. Exhausted from too many meetings and appointments; from always being on the go, frantically trying to keep up.

I pick up my soup-bowl-sized latte and sip slowly through my smirk—she hasn't yet acknowledged the fact that I'm sitting there. I patiently wait for her to look up from the screen she's pecking at with her thumbs. They move at warp speed, and I am left to assume that the novel of a text message (or email) she's composing is more important than the coffee date we've had on the calendar for a month.

I know that I have to engage; otherwise we'll still be sitting there in two separate bubbles of silence and self-absorbed space three hours later.

"Hi." I smile and offer a slight wave.

She breaks contact with her phone long enough to look up and mumble some excuse about being late (she's always late) and how she "just has to finish this quick email."

Yeah, I got it. I'm not important.

A minute passes before I make another attempt to break the awkward silence.

"How are you doing?" I offer, with a slight shake of my head and a very exasperated sigh.

"Good," she says without looking up. And then, just as I'm calculating whether or not to get up and leave her sitting alone, she places her most precious possession on the table and makes eye contact.

"Good," she repeats, "but busy." And there it is— the exasperated sigh that fills the space between us, covering everything in heaviness.

*C*hances are you've had a similar exchange with a friend— from one side of the table or the other. If you're like most people, it probably took a month to nail down the exact day and time that both of you could connect. Maybe there was a cancellation or two. Perhaps you've watched friendships fade into the background, behind all of life's other "commitments," even though that wasn't the plan, nor is it how you want to live your life. And yet, sadly, *busy* is the word we use most often when describing our lives to others.

It is the typical response between friends, colleagues, and acquaintances alike. It's as if "busy" has become the symbol of success. No longer does our education, career, relationship, or financial status offer us validation and recognition. "Busy" seems to define our lives and give them a sense of purpose.

When we peer into the life of Jesus, however, we see an individual passionately pursuing His calling yet not once complaining about being tired, burned out, or in need of a vacation to "escape" the pace of life. Not once do we hear Him categorize His life or work as "busy." It's almost as if He had the whole work/life thing handled—as if He understood the great importance of the Sabbath. (Oh, that's right—He was sitting next to His Father when that first day of rest was instituted.[23])

Right alongside "Don't kill people" and "Don't commit adultery," God gave the command for us to rest,[24] to find time in our week for life-giving activities and relationships. We are to take time to fill ourselves back up and recharge. God was specific about our need to stop working, and you can pick up several excellent titles from your favorite book retailer that explain why—and how—we need to create this rhythm in our lives. *Rhythms of Rest: Finding the Spirit of Sabbath in a Busy World* by Shelly Miller is one of my favorites, and I love the way John Mark Comer writes about Sabbath in his book *Garden City: Work, Rest, and the Art of Being Human.*

Truthfully, "rest" is a difficult concept in the modern world where our phones are the first things we check in the morning and not answering a call means losing a sale. Social media is no longer about peering into the lives of friends and family but networking and leveraging our platforms for greater influence. Coming home at 6:00 p.m. doesn't signal the cessation of work as it used to in the days of Ward Cleaver; instead, it means that we have merely changed the location of where we conduct business. The busyness is inescapable. *Supposedly.*

---

[23] Genesis 2:3 NIV

[24] Exodus 20:3–17

Even at this breakneck speed that makes the world turn these days, we don't see God changing His mind about commandment number four. He didn't allow any room for personal translations when He commanded that a day be set aside to abstain from working; His desire is for an actual "stop" to the constant busyness and striving and work. And for many of us, the stopping is a challenge because it is our desire for validation and recognition that is out of control; our striving is an issue of the heart. The trophy that we proudly carry around says "Busy," and it is our way of signaling to the world that our lives have meaning. *Because they do.*

Our lives are purposed,[25] right from the beginning.[26] Too often, however, we live as though the pursuit of that purpose is what gives us significance. Instead of recognizing our worth as being firmly grounded in our identity as God's kids, we strive to gain His affections and recognition for our accomplishments—just as we seek these things from earthly parents. I heard Bill Johnson talk about how the busyness of our lives can become artificial significance. It was a moment of clarity, and for days I sat and considered where in my life that was true for me. Was I signaling to myself (and others) that because I was "busy" I had significance? Where was I pursuing busyness but nothing of real purpose? Where was my purpose being lost in my chase after a life that looked (and felt) "busy"?

We start living with the belief that if we're not busy, then we're not doing anything noteworthy. But it isn't the busyness of our lives that makes God love us more or gives

---

[25] Jeremiah 29:11

[26] Psalm 139:13 NIV

us a better standing. He doesn't love us more when we are pushing toward our dreams. His affection toward us is the same whether we are celebrating victories or struggling in the middle of a crisis. He doesn't say, "Come to Me, and then do great things in My name." He just says, "Follow."

— — —

For many of us, the inner hustle is the most deafening noise. We don't want to admit it, and we're quick to judge others who appear to have been swept up by that movement, but inside we know the chant. It is the voice that says that productivity is next to godliness. So we fill our red cart full of planners and organizers, gel pens, highlighters, sticky notes, and an overpriced chalkboard—because it was on the endcap. We download the latest apps and spend hours charting our days, reading books from best-selling authors, and mapping out our weeks, months, and the next five years. We want to look like we've got it together and hate to admit that we lack self-discipline. We don't want anyone to know that we habitually make it to March each year in a heap of self-loathing for having failed at every one of our New Year's resolutions. *Okay, the end of January.*

For some, having a five-year plan is a terrific strategy. If a sixty-dollar planner is what you need to keep your life on track, then go for it, my friend. If you have plans to build your business, write a book, or start a ministry, chances are you need to have goals to work toward, visual reminders, actionable steps, and the accountability of a cheerleading team to maintain your momentum.

But what about the rest of us?

If you know that God has called you to embrace the

season you're in right now with young children underfoot, then why are you burning the midnight oil for things that only leave you exhausted and empty the next morning (when your family needs you to be fresh and ready to tackle the day)? If the lane God has you in is that of being a good neighbor, good wife, good student, good employee, why are you juggling two businesses and trying to become a social media superstar? If you're called to establish a business, then why are you overloading your schedule with church activities out of obligation or fear that "there is no one else" to organize the women's tea social? If God has placed it on your heart to go back to school or to work part-time at the homeless shelter in your city, then why are you signing up all three of your kids for different sports—a scheduling nightmare that will only leave you frazzled, exhausted, and with little quality time for your family?

Has the quest for a purposed life left you feeling really busy but not fulfilled? If so, there's a chance that "being busy" has become the goal you're pursuing. For some of you, perhaps busyness has become your god. It is what leaves you feeling the most fulfilled, the most valued. It's no longer your calling that is propelling you, but the validation from others that what you're "getting after" is admirable.

The following quote is from an article posted on the Grit & Virtue website, a personal development company whose purpose is to "equip women on a mission to build unstoppable momentum, become spiritually confident, and to never feel alone on the journey":

If you don't have time to do the things God has called you to do, you are doing things He didn't intend for you to do. . . . It's time to examine our schedule and decide what doesn't belong there.[27]

Our calendars tell a great deal about what is most important to us, and evaluating them can help us determine whether we're "living busy" as a way to prove our significance.

What is it that consumes the bulk of your time? Is it bolstering your social media stats? Ensuring your physical presence at every church event during the week? Are the things you feel you're supposed to be doing right now, in this season, the things that are getting the best and most of your time and energy? Or have you given in to the voice shouting, *That's not enough!* Are you productive because you have goals that honor God, goals that He has asked you to pursue, or are your days filled with a striving that amounts to nothing? Has artificial significance taken over your life?

---

[27] Christa Hutchins, "Your Calling: If You Don't Take It Seriously, No One Will," Grit & Virtue, https://gritandvirtue.com/your-calling-if-you-dont-take-it-seriously-no-one-will/.

CHAPTER 6

The Mommy Hustle

"Andrew, grab that boy! He's getting too close to Jesus!" Peter's face is crimson, as much from exhaustion as from irritation. He motions to James and John to help Thomas with the group of mothers holding babies. He already turned them away once—can't they take a hint?

"How can these people think that Jesus has time to draw up every child into His lap? Don't these parents realize that there are sick people here wanting to be healed? Can't they see that the Master is simply too busy teaching the crowds to spend time playing pat-a-cake with the toddlers?" Peter's face is contorted into a snarl as he grabs another youngster by the collar. "How does Jesus expect us to do crowd control day after day? Why doesn't He send them away? Doesn't Jesus understand that there are adults here with real problems?"

Peter keeps looking at Jesus, hoping to catch His eye and silently plead his case. He brushes a hand through his sweaty locks and exhales as, out the corner of his eye, he notices a father. With one hand, the man is holding tightly to a small girl; his other is wrapped around a babe probably only a few months old. Peter pushes past the people in front of him, making a beeline toward the father. Seething, he marches right up to him, plowing his dirty finger into the man's chest. Through bared teeth, he whispers, "Get these children out of here!" His words drip with venom. The father looks into the crazed eyes of one of Jesus' closest companions, searching for a morsel of compassion, but finding none, he turns away. He stoops to pick up his small daughter into his free arm and whispers to her in Hebrew that she won't be able to meet Jesus today. From his eyes spill tears, but his mouth turns up in a smile—he promises they will try again tomorrow.

Peter nods, feeling victorious, and turns around to scan the mob for his next victim. But standing in his shadow is Jesus, whose eyes hold a look Peter has seen before—a mix of heartache and exasperation. He places a hand on Peter's shoulder and blinks. In a single movement and without a word, Jesus steps around him and grabs both of the father's children into His capable arms. Through tears, the young father smiles into the face of the most loving person he's ever encountered and whispers his thanks.

One of the most challenging stories of the Gospels, the one that makes me cringe every time I read it, is this account of the disciples who tried to herd the children away from Jesus. They were so concerned about the little people being a nuisance to Jesus and the more important things He had on His agenda. Bless their sweet hearts for wanting to make sure that Jesus stayed on task and didn't get bogged down in details or situations that were beneath Him. Their hustling minds got them into trouble in this instance, because Jesus rebuked them sharply—telling them that unless they became like children, they would not enter the kingdom of heaven. It's an echo of Jesus' words to Martha: *"You're focused on the wrong things; slow down; trust Me; I know a better way."*

As a mother, I always find that this story hits too close to home. It's embarrassing to admit that sometimes I do this very thing. Too many times I have pushed my kids away, just as the disciples do in this story in Mark. If you're a mom or if you hang out with moms, tell me if any of these scenarios sound familiar:

- "Mommy, are you almost done with [fill in the blank]?"
- "Can you play with me?"
- "You said you were going to [fill in the blank]."
- "Put down your phone and come read to me!"

That last one was a zinger. It is verbatim from the mouth of my oldest, who was probably only a kindergartener at the time. Talk about the Holy Spirit speaking to you through your children!

You've probably heard some variation of the above lines if your children are more than two years old. And even if you're part of the small portion of society that doesn't struggle with an addiction to technology, you have your own battles. Maybe you have a career that demands your time and attention even when you are at home, and you find yourself echoing the disciples' response: "Go away, kids. Mommy has more important things to do." Perhaps the side-hustle business you said would consume only "nights and weekends" is now reaching its fingers into the daytime hours to the point where your kids get parked in front of the TV for long stretches of time. For some, the all-consuming distraction may be a hobby, something creative you're passionate about, or even a ministry opportunity that began as a part-time commitment but has blown up into something more demanding.

Any of these things can be the best idea, work, or opportunity. You can be operating in your natural abilities or spiritual gifts or pursuing that career that you went into six-figure debt for. It is admirable and amazing that mothers of young children would have the energy to engage in anything beyond full-time parenting. Please hear my heart: I am in no way condemning the hard work of moms. What I am challenging is the chant of the hustling heart—the voice that says your children are the distraction and the other thing demanding your time is the most important thing. Because it isn't.

At the end of the day, when we are showered with awards as a top-tier saleswoman for a multilevel marketing company with the most honorable mission statement out there but we have ruined our relationship with our children in the process, will the success be worth it? If our businesses, social platforms, or ministries give us influence over thousands or millions of people but we have lost the respect and affection of our children, what have we truly gained? If we can purchase for our kids all the toys and gadgets they could want and take them on all kinds of exotic vacations but are unable to have honest communication with them, will the money mean anything? If we have lost the ability to shepherd their hearts, dialogue with them, and say, "Follow me, as I follow Jesus," then what is it we have so willingly given ourselves to?

Our role as parents is to teach and train our children in the ways of the Lord so that they will know which paths to take in life.[28] Even if we disciple hundreds of people, our most monumental impact will be on the hearts of our children. We are the ones who will tell them how much God adores them and what great pleasure He takes in them. We are the first to speak words of life over them; it is our arms that hold them, providing comforting shelter and tender love. In every way, we are their first glimpse of the love of God and His great affection for them.

So what happens when the gentleness of Jesus clashes with what our kids hear from us? Do they know that they are more significant than our screens, clients, bosses, followers, friends, goals, bodies, and even our dreams? As adults, we're insulted when people choose to be head-down on their devices instead of engaged in conversation with us, whether we're sitting in the same room or on the other side of a table. How much more does gaze aversion send a message to our children that some things in our lives are more important to us than they are?

Peter saw the children's desire for Jesus' time and attention as trivial. He overlooked them as little people and saw only their neediness. But nothing moves the heart of Jesus more than people with needs. He can't help but stop. His heart burns, and His head swivels in an instant when the needy cry out to Him. It is His nature to pause. Even if only for one person. No one was too small, too insignificant, too needy for Jesus.

Regardless of what is competing with our children for

---

[28] Proverbs 22:6

our time and attention, I believe Jesus' response would be the same: "Don't push these children away. Don't ever get between them and me. These children are at the very center of life in the kingdom."[29]

While I love my children, I would be lying if I said I love being with them 100 percent of the time. I've come to embrace my current season as a full-time, homeschooling mother, but there are also many days when the closest public school looks appealing—if only for the seven hours it would allot me to enjoy some peace and quiet and get errands done on my own. I am not supermom. None of us are.

But Jesus, in His compelling but tender way, presses our hearts toward a better version of the parent-child relationship. He didn't view children as an inconvenience, nuisance, chore, or responsibility, as I tend to at times. They were worthy of His time, love, and affection. I picture Him walking with the disciples from one place to the next with a constant buzz of children around Him. They are playing and running, pushing past others to be near Him, to hold His hand, to feel His embrace, to catch a glimpse of His loving smile.

Jesus' warning to the disciples (and all who heard His voice) was that we are to come to Him like children—with wonder and humility. Without pretense and insecurity. Eager to learn, to be with Him, to ask silly questions, to delight in His presence—just as our children often are with us. Jesus was reminding them, again, that relationships are always the more important thing. The woman at the

---

[29] Mark 10:14 MSG

well, Zacchaeus, the bleeding woman, Lazarus, the blind man, the paralyzed man, the man with leprosy, the demon-possessed man—each was worth His time. They were worth the interruption, worth the effort, worth whatever others might think or say about Him. People were the most pressing thing to Jesus.

Repeat this with me: "Relationships are *always* the more important thing."

Why do our children have to compete for our time, attention, and energy next to our best friends, church, and career? At the end of our lives, will we wish we'd lived in a cleaner house or that we'd spent more time playing in forts on rainy days with our kids? When we are old and wrinkled, will we fret over the saggy skin and extra weight or be concerned with the kind of legacy we are leaving behind? Will we lament over not consuming enough kale or that we didn't celebrate every milestone with cake and ice cream? Will we care that our kids weren't Einstein scholars as long as they grow to be adults who are confident in their identity as God's kids? If we build the most profitable business, the most extensive network, or the most recognizable brand but fail to spark in our children a love for God, His Word, and His people, then what will it matter? Relationships are the most important thing. Always.

CHAPTER 7

Close to Jesus Yet Still Hustling

*P*eter, Andrew, James, John, Philip, Bartholomew, Thomas, Matthew, James, Thaddeus, Simon, and Judas. These were the names of the apostles. The twelve disciples of Jesus. The dozen men who traveled with, lived with, and had a front-row seat to the miracles and mystery of God incarnate.

They were the very first believers—the bona fide followers of Jesus—those willing to drop their livelihood and kiss their families goodbye. They were quick to respond to the voice of Jesus and, except for Judas, spent the rest of their days devoted to Him. After He left, they took on the responsibility of spreading the Good News throughout the world. The early church was built on the shoulders of these men, a result of their hard work. We esteem them. They get the highest place of honor, and we tend to fight against jealousy when we consider the proximity they had to Jesus—three whole years face-to-face with the Son of God. (I'm getting goose bumps just writing these lines!)

Yet for the pedestal that they are placed on, these twelve were simple, ordinary men. There wasn't anything special about them or anything extraordinary about what they had to offer. What motivated their heroic actions had little to do with who they were but everything to do with the One whom they followed. It was Jesus who compelled them to such greatness—not anything they possessed on their own.

Because of the disciples' closeness to Jesus, most people wouldn't describe them as hustlers. Several of them were humble fishermen—blue-collar workers. Even Matthew, with his tax-collecting days in the past, was not concerned about acquiring anything for himself once he decided to follow Jesus. Still, there was an ongoing conversation among this crew, and it's similar to one we hear today.

There was a definite preoccupation with personal position and advancement even within the "inner circle of three" (Peter, James, and John). We read in the book of Mark about James and John demanding a place of honor next to Jesus when He sat on His throne in heaven.[30] Matthew records that James and John's mother came to Jesus on her knees, begging the same thing.[31] Of course, there would be jealousy and dissension among the ranks when the rest of the disciples learned of this conversation, and maybe that was why Peter seemed to be so concerned with what Jesus had planned for John. Perhaps you can recall Peter's final conversation with Jesus, where he asked point blank, "What's going to happen to him?"[32]

We can all find some camaraderie among the disciples who were casting side-glances, wondering if they were being crowded out. Our preoccupation with what others have, or have been called to, often sounds like this:

- "Why can't I have the gift that so-and-so has?"
- "How is it that my friend is doing _____, but I have to _____?"

[30] Mark 10:35–37

[31] Matthew 20:20-21

[32] John 21:20–22

Other times we can be found running and pushing ourselves past others like Peter, eager to get to Jesus *first* and prove our perfect love for Him.[33]

— — —

Often at the front of the Twelve (and continuously striving for that position) was Peter. He wanted to be the leader of the pack and was quick to show Jesus just how capable and committed he was to their cause (even when he wasn't able to fully articulate that cause). Peter's zealous personality was matched only by his prideful heart. I can identify with all of those character flaws as well as the fact that his words tended to get him into trouble. He was always inserting his foot into his mouth to the point where Jesus once rebuked him, saying, "Get away from me, Satan! . . . You are seeing things merely from a human point of view, not from God's."[34]

It sounds harsh, and it no doubt cut Peter deeply. More times than not, we see things merely from a human point of view and not from God's. Perhaps you're like Peter (and myself), and you've actually been so brazen as to tell God how things *really* are, as if His perspective isn't as clear as yours.

The story of Peter cutting off the ear of the temple guard in the Garden of Gethsemane is a favorite for me.[35] I'm not sure what he was thinking, because Jesus had never once talked about leading the charge to change the world with force and military tactics. His words were always about loving your enemy and praying for those who

---

[33] John 20:3–8

[34] Mark 8:33 NLT

[35] John 18:10–11

persecute you,[36] promoting peace,[37] and turning the other cheek.[38] *Surely someone else noticed when he picked up his sword and started swinging. Why didn't anyone stop him? Jesus, why did You allow that to happen?*

Regardless of why, Jesus did allow Peter to cut off the man's ear—just as He allowed Judas to betray Him and lead the guards right into their prayer meeting. He permitted His betrayer to stand face-to-face with Him and plant a kiss on His cheek—*talk about being bold, Judas!*

But once Peter swung and blood was gushing from the guard's head, Jesus commanded those who were bent on fighting to stop.[39] By this point, the disciples (Peter especially) would have been used to Jesus' reprimanding tone. It's the next part of the story that brings me to tears—the swift and purposeful movements of Jesus. In an instant, Jesus lifted His hand to cover the damage that Peter had caused.

How often do we tend to make a mess when we operate out of our finite wisdom and eagerness to do what we think God wants us to do? Jesus didn't condemn Peter or embarrass him there in front of all his friends, though He could have. Jesus didn't stop to give a sermon or ask the guard with a dangling ear if he would like to repent of his sins. He moved quickly to heal and restore; Jesus made the man's ear like new.[40]

How glad I am that God still does the same thing

---

[36] Matthew 5:44

[37] Matthew 5:9

[38] Matthew 5:39

[39] Luke 22:51

[40] Luke 22:51

today: covering the damage we've created due to our hustling hearts. When we charge forward with our own agenda (like Peter, wielding a weapon because he thought that was the only way), we do damage; we hurt others—physically, emotionally, and spiritually. We neglect those we love in an attempt to "provide for" them or climb the ladder of success. We demand results and timelines from team members and friends without thinking about the ramifications of our taskmaster behavior. We pick up our "sword" and wave it around, spewing verses that cut people deeply, because while they may be full of truth, they are void of love. We defend Jesus because we think that's our job, but it isn't—just as it wasn't Peter's place to do so. Jesus never asked the disciples to defend Him; He simply called them to follow.

— — —

Right before Jesus ascended into heaven, He gave His followers a final set of instructions. They were explicit; He left no room for interpretation. He said, "Stay here in the city until he [the Holy Spirit] arrives, until you're equipped with power from on high."[41]

I wonder why Jesus was so specific about His followers waiting in Jerusalem until they had received the Holy Spirit. It was as if He knew what would have happened if they went to preach the Gospel and baptize the nations in their own strength.[42] Was it their motives that most concerned Him? Surely not. They had witnessed incredible miracles and indeed had good news to share with

---

[41] Luke 24:49 MSG

[42] Mark 16:15

the world; their desire to make Jesus known was pure and sincere.

What Jesus knew was that they were powerless to carry out His commands on their own. They needed the partnership of the Holy Spirit to accomplish the task before them. So while His directive was to go and do, they first needed to sit and wait.

That line is hard for us to digest. It's easy for us to rally around the idea of "doing" something. But the idea of "waiting" leaves us uncomfortable. It forces us to sit with our thoughts and inadequacies; to recognize that even the greatest of ideas, the strongest of work ethics, if carried out in our own way or in our own time, won't be as effective as when we partner with God—relying on His strength to give us the power we need. We don't tend to see the delay as a good thing. Many of us get excited about our dreams and march off in our own strength with our own ideas, gifts, and gumption to achieve them, without first waiting on God.

For some of you reading, the opposite may be more accurate. Sometimes we have been given marching orders to go but are still sitting comfortably on our bottoms waiting. Friend, let me be clear: if God has told you what to do, then you'd better get after it. Sin is knowing the good you ought to do and *not* doing it.[43] But I digress.

Back to the disciples, waiting together, curious as to what would happen next. Would the Holy Spirit be there for them the way Jesus had been? I'm sure their hearts and minds and conversations were full of wondering and

---

[43] James 4:17 NIV

assumptions. But then He came in power, and there was evidence of His presence,[44] and the church was never the same.

Now when Peter went into the city and met the lame man, he would have the power to command the man to "get up, and roll up your sleeping mat!"[45] There was no longer the toil of trying to do something in his ability alone. The words he spoke contained an authority that Peter never could have attained in a lifetime of hustling. He was not acting out of his agenda; his mission wasn't to build anything glorious for his name. Peter was doing what Jesus had commanded him to do. He was moving in God's time frame (after waiting patiently) and in the power of the Holy Spirit. His purpose was to make the name of Jesus known, and because of that, God gave Peter great influence. He didn't have to hustle and strive for it. It happened because he had surrendered his heart; he was eager to move with God when God said to go.

---

[44] Acts 2

[45] Acts 9:34 NLT

CHAPTER 8

The Church Hustle

*J*ust throw yourself out there. . ."

She continued with her story, but my mind was stuck on those five words. We kept walking while she talked, but internally I was ten paces behind, trying to let her statement settle someplace in my heart. It was a beautiful morning in early summer; the kids were walking and riding scooters next to us, dodging the other runners and dog walkers at the lake that day. The sun was overhead, heating up the water; the clouds covered us just so—everything was perfect.

But inside my heart, storm clouds were starting to form as I digested this woman's advice. The words felt sharp as they churned over and over in my mind. To be honest, I was struggling to keep up with where the conversation had moved. We had been talking about church and where I wanted to be involved. She had asked about my previous leadership experience and what things stirred my heart. She was the elder of the two of us, and after telling her story and sharing her experience, she advised me to do what she had done and "throw myself out there."

We had just moved. To a new city, a new state, a new church, and new jobs. We had no family, no friends, no connections whatsoever to this place where we had just landed, and I knew I needed to find community—fast. As a mother of young children, I needed friends who would understand my current season of life (the exhaustion from chasing toddlers all day and surviving on dinosaur-shaped food). I needed an outlet for my creativity, and my natural tendency was to "get involved" at church. My husband had a built-in set of budding relationships within his colleague pool, but I was going to bed at night feeling isolated in this new place. I was excited about our new adventure, but even in the midst of the thrill of new beginnings, her counsel was crushing. I knew my current season of life wouldn't allow me the luxury of jumping into multiple service and volunteer opportunities; it just wasn't feasible.

I was not a young single with endless hours of free time. My children were not yet in school full-time, nor would they be for several years. I was still in the throes of nap schedules and diapers, tantrums and play dates. I didn't have the spare room in our budget to allow for a nanny, even though that was the norm for our new zip code, and neither did I want to pay for child care so that I could volunteer at church.

While a younger and much more naive version of myself may have jumped at the suggestion to "throw myself out there," I confidently left the conversation knowing that was precisely *not* what I was planning to do. A few years earlier, I would have heeded the advice and then struggled under the onslaught of guilt from having abandoned my two young children. My reality was that my kids were my priority, not serving in the church. I knew myself well enough to know that working in the preschool ministry or stapling together workbooks for some random ministry meeting would not leave me feeling fulfilled. I also knew that being present for my family, at home, was my priority. *Homeschool* was a word I was hearing more and more often, and I felt that perhaps it was the direction the Lord was pointing me in. I knew I wouldn't be able to "do it all" well, and so I opted to do nothing. I didn't get involved in women's ministry. I didn't join a Bible study or life group right away. My home was my first circle of influence: loving and supporting my husband in his new job and being fully present for my children. After that, my goal was to get to know our neighbors and love them well.

It seems so simple to admit it now; perhaps a little too simple. And yet in that season, I remember feeling judged for not "serving" or volunteering more. I can recall the weight of comments such as, "We want you to be more involved," from well-meaning church leaders and wondering what exactly that meant. *When did being present for my family become less important than being present for women's Bible study?*" I wrote in my journal. This was the first time I felt the pressure of the church hustle.

Chances are, if you've been around the church world for longer than a week, you've experienced something similar: the encouragement to "get involved," "volunteer," or "use your gifts" in the church. These words can be laid down condescendingly or subtly implied, but the idea they convey is that to be a mature believer, you need to fill your schedule with church activities—even if you're *already* volunteering at your child's school, at the neighborhood theater, as a soccer coach, or at Boy Scouts. It doesn't matter if you're hosting weekly neighborhood BBQs, facilitating playdates with other moms, or delivering meals to those who just had a baby or lost a loved one. The underlying message is, "If it isn't a church-related ministry, then it doesn't count." But that is a lie.

It was in those first few months after moving that I realized I could give in to this idea, this pressure to "be a part of" something, or I could lean in for a greater understanding of what God wanted me to do in that season of my life. I grew confident in my discovery that God doesn't call us all to do the same thing at the same time. What is a priority for someone else doesn't have to be mine. What others are giving themselves to in their homes, families, businesses, creatively, or online doesn't have to dictate what I spend my days doing. We need to be careful that what everyone else thinks is a worthwhile use of their time and talents doesn't drown out what God is asking us to do. We need to listen intently for the voice of the Holy Spirit and move confidently in the direction He's leading—even if it's not what others recommend or even ask us to do.

- - -

Just this week I was invited by someone to join a team at our church. It was a great opportunity to serve, especially since I am, again, in a new city and chapter of life. The person asking was fairly influential, and I was surprised when my initial response was, "No," without missing a beat. I smiled, knowing my decisive answer meant growth, that I had matured past the people-pleasing self that would have jumped at the opportunity to serve in any capacity, especially when a well-respected person asked. Instead, I took twenty-four hours to see if my immediate response was what God was approving or whether this was an area He wanted me to submit to, because to be honest, it wasn't something I necessarily wanted to do.

In the end, I told this person, "Not right now," after taking a night to sleep on it and discussing the invitation with my husband. I knew that saying no meant I might not be asked to join anything else for a while, and I was comfortable with that. Saying no to this opportunity *could* make me look unspiritual, *could* offend the person who asked, *could* isolate me, but I was confident in my understanding of what God was calling me to do right then, regardless of how it *appeared* to others. I was done having to qualify my yeses and nos; I was secure, knowing my worth isn't dictated by how others perceive me or what they want me to be. I was giving up the hustle for approval and recognition.

- - -

It has taken me years to get better at coming to God and asking Him about ideas rather than demanding His blessing on my own concocted plans. I've learned to come with open hands and a humble heart, asking Him, "Is this what You want me to do?" rather than expecting Him to jump and grant His favor to my every request. Part of that lesson is learning to wait—listening for His gentle voice and not rushing the conversation. I love the way Joanna Gaines describes her interactions with the Lord in her book *The Magnolia Story*. She writes about the back-and-forth conversation she had with God about reopening her shop in Waco after having closed it to tend to her family. Her admission that she tends to argue with God *at first* was particularly comforting—showing me that I'm not the only one who summons such courage when talking with God. She describes God's voice not as booming or thunderous but as more of a whisper, and shares that she felt peace when she finally chose to obey. I remember closing my eyes and smiling as I finished reading that particular story, knowing well the warm-blanket feeling of God's peace. I too have come to appreciate the peacefulness of surrendering my plans and fully embracing what God is asking me to do—even when that means saying no to someone.

Perhaps this is a new concept for you—that you don't have to say yes to every request from every leader, pastor, mentor, or friend. I hope your heart is hearing the beat of that freedom. Friend, if you're in a similar season with young children underfoot, then dive deep into the grace pool and take a lap. Get comfortable with the idea that your family is your priority and that saying no is perfectly acceptable if that's what God is speaking to your heart.

Even if your house is void of children, you, friend, still may need this assurance: the church won't fall apart if you aren't leading everywhere. Maybe you're in school and recognize that maintaining your GPA requires your full attention, or maybe you're caring for an ailing family member or slogging your way through the paperwork for adoption. Perhaps your husband is in a season of building his career, developing a business, or launching a church. You have a vision for what your life is supposed to look like *right now*, and you've immersed yourself fully. Don't let anyone derail you! Keep going! Do the work. Get after the things God has called you to!

Let's be believers whose yeses mean "yes" and whose nos mean "no"[46]—not caving to please others, manipulating situations for our glory, or serving out of obligation.[47] And while we're at it, let's stop feeling guilty for choosing family over ministry.

---

[46] Matthew 5:37

[47] Colossians 3:23

CHAPTER 9

Eve's FOMO (Fear of Missing Out)

The voice of the Snake is gentle; his opening remarks straightforward and seemingly harmless. With a whisper, he weaves doubt and fear into a shawl and then gracefully drapes it over Eve's shoulders. She glances at Adam, who is happily tending to the animals just a stone's throw away, and then looks longingly at the fruit dangling from the heavily laden branch.

"Surely God won't kill you for eating this fruit," the Snake scoffs with a smirk. "Will God really notice? He has provided it for you; He's the One who put it here in your garden."

Eve reaches out her hand but then quickly retracts it, her mind divided on whether to obey God's command or give in to her curiosity. The Snake slithers closer, continuing to spew lies in her direction.

"Why can't you just try some? Did God really say you couldn't have any of it?" he asks in a slick voice. "Doesn't God want you to be wiser?" he mocks. "Will He really know if you take just one piece of fruit?"

The banter plays over and over inside her head. The Snake seems so sure and his arguments so fair. Eve teeters on the edge of her life-altering decision for what feels like an eternity, while the Snake coils at her feet. And then in an instant, everything changes. Her hand pulls the fruit from the limb, her lips caress *its flesh, and her tongue tastes truth. Her eyes fly wide open as her heart plummets into darkness.*

Evil laughter rings out. Slinking into the shadow beneath the tree, the Snake roars with delight at the thought that he has ruined God's perfection. He has successfully turned these creatures, man, against their Maker. And how? With a simple whisper:

"You can have more."

"It's sitting right there, available for you."

"Take the easy way."

"You can have it all."

"You can be anything you want."

The Snake's words to Eve sound a lot like the chant of the hustling heart: *"Did God really tell you to be quiet, to sit still, to give away your money, to sow your greatest talents into that church? Doesn't God want you to do more and be more and have more than what you have right now?"*

The cunning whisper of a fallen angel, the one who speaks nothing but lies, is quick to spin doubt—in ourselves and in God. The garden is where the idea of wanting more first came into being, with Satan's devious lips promising Eve that something better was waiting on the other side of the fruit. The Liar whispered to her that what God had given her access to wasn't the best, that she was missing out, that she had a right to attain what she wanted at any cost—even if it meant disobeying God.

The bite of the forbidden fruit was the first act of disobedience in the history of man. It was also the first act based on FOMO (fear of missing out). Eve's decision shows that we can have whatever we desire if only we are willing to break a rule—or a relationship.

Most of us have succumbed to this feeling. We read someone's latest social media post or scroll through images realizing that what they have is what we lack. Our blood pressure skyrockets as we compare our real life to the highlight reels of our friends (online or in real life). We feel that we "have" to have what others are talking about, buying, or doing, or we risk being left behind. We live with the belief that God made a mistake and gave what we deserve to someone else: her body, husband, opportunity, or gift. We are no longer content because the Enemy has done his job of constructing lies built on confusion, envy, and panic. The "keep up with the Joneses" song plays on repeat, in stereo, every day.

Starting in the garden and all throughout scripture, we watch as others get swept into the lie that God is holding out, that He doesn't want us to have success, or that we have to "do" something to hurry His hand. Abraham and Sarah, Rebekah and Jacob, Joseph, Aaron and Miriam, Absalom, and half the kings found in the Old Testament all connived and twisted God's promises to achieve their own purpose. The fear of missing out is not a modern problem.

Rather than confidently moving the direction that God asks us to move, we tend to get distracted by what everyone else is doing. We forget what God has spoken to us and instead question why we can't have what others do. We challenge God's motives and timing, claiming that He is either late or not concerned with helping us fulfill our purpose. In our impatience, we angrily shake a fist at God and walk away with a toddler-sized pout. We probably sound a lot like Peter, who, though he was in the midst of an intimate conversation with Jesus, was preoccupied with someone else's future:

> *Peter turned and saw the follower Jesus loved very much walking behind them. (This was the follower who had leaned against Jesus at the supper and said, "Lord, who is it that will hand you over?") When Peter saw him behind them, he asked Jesus, "Lord, what about him?"*[48]

Though it seems Peter was focused on the words of Jesus, it's evident that he missed just how critical the moment was. Not only had Jesus pulled Peter away from the rest of the disciples for a private conversation, but He had covered Peter's past sin with grace and mercy. Jesus decided to reinstate Peter (in spite of his recent denial) as one of the key leaders of His ministry and movement. He was setting Peter up to be one of the great fathers of the early church![49] This tender moment was one that other men dreamed of, and yet all that Peter was concerned with was what Jesus was going to say to John. Because of his fear of missing out, he didn't recognize the moment for what it was. And I wonder: How many moments do we miss for the exact same reason?

I love that Jesus gives us second chances—and third, and fourth, and on and on. I love that He doesn't hold our past against us but pulls us up after we fall and clothes us with tenderness and mercy. And I love that sometimes

[48] John 21:20–21 ERV

[49] Matthew 16:18

Jesus takes off the kid gloves with Peter (I feel like I'm in good company when it seems He's taken them off with me). In essence what Jesus says to Peter is, *"Don't worry about John! You do what I've asked. Get after the task I just gave you, Peter, and don't get distracted by what others are doing."* It sounds rather familiar: *"Malinda, don't concern yourself with what I've asked her to do." "Don't worry about what gift she has received." "Haven't I given you a job to do?" "Are you going to obey Me or fixate on what someone else is doing?"*

And my question to you, reader, is this: Are you working hard toward what God has asked *you* to do? Or are you hustling toward something that hasn't been asked of you because you feel like you deserve it, need it, or just plain want it? Have you become distracted and concerned with what others are doing? Are you stuck on the hamster wheel of comparing and complaining? Are you listening to the lies telling you that what you have right now isn't enough, that you deserve more, that God messed up somehow?

— — —

Not too long ago I heard a speaker talk about how jealousy is rooted in the belief that God doesn't have enough to go around. It took about a millisecond for the words to pierce my heart. It was like this man had read my journals, which brimmed with questions hurled at God. I wanted to know why others were dancing in success at the top of the mountain while I was slowly struggling uphill and feeling like I was falling backward with every other step. The jealousy wasn't overt—I was still cheering on my peers who were achieving success and fulfilling their goals. Honestly, I was happy for them, but I wasn't able to separate their accomplishments from my lack. My jealousy sprang from my fear of missing out.

Jealousy says, *"Someone else has achieved it, so I can't."*

It whispers, *"She's already attained success, so why bother trying."*

It insists, *"You have to do this now, or you're going to be left behind."*

It chants, *"Why aren't you running like her, selling like her, doing _____ like her?"*

It is the same old lie from the garden, spun into a different web, but still as deadly. It places our wisdom above God's, demanding that He act when we command. We feel the need to remind Him, repeatedly, that what *He promised* us hasn't yet come to pass, as though the God of the universe needs accountability to do what He said He'd do. We bring our tally sheets to Him in tears, noting what He's done for others and not for us. We are quick to list His promises and point out how He's slacking in fulfilling them, even though on the opposite side of the equation are terms that we haven't fully upheld.

> *What you commanded, I've done. I haven't detoured around your commands, I haven't forgotten a single one. . . . I have listened obediently to the Voice of GOD, my God, I have lived the way you commanded me.*[50]

This verse from Deuteronomy makes me uncomfortable. It paints a picture very unlike the life I live at times. Does it sound like an accurate description of your life? Have you

---

[50] Deuteronomy 26:13–14 MSG

listened obediently to the voice of God and lived the way He has asked you to? Or is the fear of missing out pushing you and pulling you away from what you know you're supposed to be doing? Have you finished what God told you to do, or did you start out well but then get distracted? Have you abandoned the plan He laid out for you, walking away from the people and purposes that once weighed on your heart so heavily?

The fear of missing out is rooted in doubt that God can actually do what He says He can do. We assume that God has only one way of doing things or that because something hasn't happened *yet*, it never will. Don't let jealousy rob you of contentment and joy. Don't let fear creep in and distract you when God has spoken plainly. Choose to believe that God's timing is best, even if His plan doesn't happen the way you assume it will. In my experience, God's timing is always best—even if He tends to operate in a time zone far different than our own.

PART ONE:

Reflection and Small Group Questions

The following pages are here for your personal reflection or small group study. The questions are meant to spark introspection and to propel you into a deeper relationship with Jesus. Please don't rush through the questions, but take your time to consider them, answering with honesty and courage. (Your knee-jerk response may not be the most genuine, so give yourself time to work through the material.)

My prayer is that you would enter each moment of journaling and discussion with this prayer on your lips: "Father, help me to hear Your voice, to know Your presence, and to move in the direction You're leading me." May it be the thought that you return to with each set of questions, and may taking this time to probe your heart and mind truly bring you closer to Jesus.

CHAPTER 1: THIS THING CALLED HUSTLE

Where have you felt the chant of "hustle" in your own life? *(List all the areas: at work, in your parenting, at school, on social media, at church, regarding your health/fitness, etc.)*

Do you find yourself giving in to the hustle through perfectionism or people pleasing?

Who is it that you feel you need to impress?

Are there areas where the lines between building your own empire and building God's kingdom have been blurred?

What are you going to do about it?

Who can you turn to for accountability if this is something you struggle with?

What healthy boundaries can you create so that you stay focused on your goal without losing your soul?

Take some time to read these verses (perhaps in several different translations) and listen for what God has to say to you:

- Colossians 3:23
- Galatians 1:10

Consider/discuss this thought: *"In our me-centered world where we believe we can become anything we set our minds to and attain anything we feel we deserve, it is no longer enough to just put a lot of effort into our work—we have to hustle after it."*

CHAPTER 2: SUFFOCATING UNDER THE HUSTLE

Have you ever compared hustle to workaholism?

Define what it means to be a workaholic.

Do you know someone you'd characterize as a "workaholic"? What is it like to be around, work for/with, or live with that person?

Read Matthew 6:33 and ask God to show you where you've been seeking other things instead of Him first.

Read Nehemiah 5:2–9 and Ecclesiastes 2:23. Which words are more comforting to you?

Is the idea of obedience as a lifestyle a new concept for you? What do you think that could look like?

Read Ecclesiastes 9:10. What does this verse mean to you?

Consider/discuss this thought: *"Stop confusing the building of your own following with the building of the church. Stop selling yourself in the name of Jesus—even if that is the popular advice shared by experts and modeled by leaders."*

CHAPTER 3: BUT DIDN'T GOD INSTITUTE HARD WORK?

Did you grow up with a healthy understanding of what "hard work" looks like? Describe what hard work looks like to you today.

Do you need to get better at working hard, or do you need to create healthier boundaries?

Are you partnering with God or merely asking Him to bless the work you're putting your hand to?

Read Matthew 25:14–30. What gift (ability/resource) has God placed in your hand?

How are you stewarding it?

What could you do to steward it better?

Consider this thought: *"God will hold us accountable for what He has given us to steward. It is only in partnership with God that the remarkable happens."* What does it look like for you to "partner" with God?

Consider/discuss this thought: *"We cross the threshold between working hard and being a workaholic when the need to work comes at the expense of other things."*

CHAPTER 4: THE BETTER THING

In what ways do you identify with Martha? With Mary?

Read Luke 10:38–42. Have you ever felt that God was saying to you, *"You're missing it. You're doing too much; your priorities are messed up, and you need to refocus"*?

What part of your life was God addressing, and how did you respond?

What happened (good or bad) as a result of your response?

What are the "better" things that God has put in your life for you to focus on right now?

How are you going to ensure these things remain your priority?

Read Matthew 6:21. What things do you treasure?

Has your hustle ever been "in God's name" and you've wanted to feel justified for all the hard work you've been doing? Be honest.

Consider this thought: *"God isn't going to ask you to sacrifice healthy relationships to pursue His purpose for your life."* Do you agree?

Can you think of any relationships that may have become strained because of your focus on something else? What steps can you take to begin mending those relationships?

What else have you sacrificed in your "doing" or in trying to do "all the things"?

CHAPTER 5: ARTIFICIAL SIGNIFICANCE

Consider this thought: *"It isn't the pursuit of our purpose that gives us significance; it's God."* Are you guilty of pursuing your purpose instead of the One who gave it to you in the first place?

Read the following passages: Matthew 18:12; Matthew 10:29–31; and Genesis 1:27. Take a moment to ask God how He sees you, and then write it down.

What pictures come to mind?

What word is He speaking over you?

Ask God to give you a fresh perspective of what it means to be His kid, with eternal significance.

Read Deuteronomy 5:12–14; Mark 6:31; and Mark 2:27. Have you ever considered that what you are striving toward is *artificial significance*?

Has the pursuit of appearing productive taken over your life?

Have you lost your joy in the midst of your busyness?

Where has your life become busy but not necessarily more significant?

Is "Sabbath" something you practice regularly? (Not just

going to church or having a day to catch up, run errands, or do household chores.)

How can you create more time for rest in your week—not just ceasing from work but engaging in things that are restful for your spirit, mind, and body?

CHAPTER 6: THE MOMMY HUSTLE

"Relationships are always the most important thing." Does this statement reflect your life—your calendar and pocketbook?

Take time to ask your spouse, children, and closest friends to answer whether they feel as important to you as other things in your life.

How do their responses make you feel?

Commit to making time to repair any relationships that are broken or in need of quality time.

Ask for forgiveness and create a plan so that the people closest to you aren't being sacrificed on the altar of your work.

Read Mark 10:13–16. Take a moment to consider whether your children would describe themselves as a distraction.

If you're not a parent, apply the same consideration to your friends or extended family members.

Consider the wisdom from Colossians 3:21; Ephesians 6:4; and Psalm 127:3–5.

Consider/discuss the following quote:

"At the end of our lives, will we wish we'd lived in a cleaner house or that we'd spent more time playing in forts on rainy days with our kids? When we are old and wrinkled, will we fret over the saggy skin and extra weight or be concerned with the kind of legacy we are leaving behind? Will we care that our kids weren't Einstein scholars as long as they grow to be adults who are confident in their identity as God's kids? If we build the most profitable business, the most extensive network, or the most recognizable brand but fail to spark in our children a love for God, His Word, and His people, then what will it matter?"

CHAPTER 7: CLOSE TO JESUS YET STILL HUSTLING

Read the following verses: Proverbs 11:2; Luke 14:11; and James 4:6.

What does it look like to "walk in humility"?

In what areas of life do you find yourself caught in comparison, always asking God about "the other person," as Peter did?

Read Matthew 20:20–23 and John 20:3–8.

How (and where) have you sought a place of importance with God?

Where are you trying to prove your worth to Him (or your righteousness to others)?

Consider/discuss this quote: *We pick up our 'sword' and wave it around, spewing verses that cut people deeply, because while they may be full of truth, they are void of love.*

Have you ever come to Jesus' defense as Peter thought he had to?

What was the result?

Were any relationships damaged as a result of wielding your sword?

Has God asked you to "sit and wait" in this season?

Have you been doing anything but?

What steps can you take to intentionally sit still today?

Consider asking someone to hold you accountable to complete the action steps you came up with.

Chapter 8: The Church Hustle

Read Ecclesiastes 3. What season are you in right now?

Are you the person who says yes to everybody, "throwing yourself out there" and burning out or becoming bitter in the process?

What things/areas do you know *right now* that you need to say no to or step away from?

Read Matthew 5:33–37. Consider what you've been asked to do by God (not by others) in your current season of life.

Write it out, no matter how small the details, and then commit to working hard at those things. (Put these priorities somewhere you'll be reminded of them often.)

Has being present for your church become more of a priority than being present for your family?

Consider/discuss this thought: *"We need to be careful that what everyone else thinks is a worthwhile use of their time and talents doesn't drown out what God is asking us to do. We need to listen intently for the voice of the Holy Spirit and move confidently in the direction He's leading—even if it's not what others recommend or even ask us to do."*

Read Luke 6:37. Has anyone ever made you feel guilty for prioritizing family (or your neighbors, friends, or personal ministry) over church?

Seek God's guidance and wisdom for where your priorities should be.

Chapter 9: Eve's FOMO (Fear of Missing Out)

Did you hear yourself in any of Eve's arguments while reading this chapter?

Where do you notice the fear of missing out (FOMO) driving your decisions?

Take time to read the following passages: John 10:10 and Deuteronomy 28:1–12.

"Jealousy is rooted in the belief that God doesn't have enough to go around." Do you agree?

If so, where do you see traces of this (false) belief in your thoughts/life?

Have there been moments when you wanted to be happy for a friend's success but jealousy choked out your excitement?

Read Philippians 2:3. What did you think about as you read these words?

Is the idea that God is "abundant" difficult for you to grasp? Why?

Read Ephesians 3:20. Explain what this means to you.

Consider/discuss these questions: *"Have you become distracted and concerned with what others are doing? Are you stuck on the hamster wheel of comparing and complaining? Are you listening to the lies telling you that what you have right now isn't enough, that you deserve more, that God messed up somehow?"*

PART TWO

Choosing Obedience

Chapter 10

What Happened to Obedience?

God, how can I?"

My pen felt heavy as I blocked and then shaded the simple words. The single question mark turned into two, then three. And suddenly there were four, five, six giant swirls of doubt-filled punctuation lining the top of the page. I glared at the remark and with a groan put my pen back to the paper. Within seconds, my thoughts blazed off across the page with no intention of slowing. From deep in the caverns of my heart came murmurs of uncertainty, fear, and insecurity. The only pause in their free-flow outpouring came when I needed to wipe the snot dangling from the end of my nose—tear-soaked pages were acceptable, but mucus-streaked? Not in the least!

Ten minutes later I was peering through swollen eyes at the words I had just scribbled, each one jumping to slap me in the face with accusations—painful and true.

"I have no experience. I have no degree. My following is small. My platform is smaller."

I blinked my eyes, surprised at the magnitude of my tear reserves.

"There are others more qualified, more eloquent, more experienced," the arguments persisted.

"I need connections but have none. What can I truly offer? Write a book? You can't be serious!"

After reading it back, I felt even worse because I knew

it was true. Every word. It was humiliating and shocking to admit my lack of courage, especially as someone who had been labeled "brave" for almost her entire life. But not now. Alone in my room, with soggy tissues covering my bed, I felt small, anonymous, and insignificant. I fell back and crossed my arms over my face to muffle an angry sob. It hung in the air above me with a smirk that said, *"You should just give up now."*

But the whisper in my heart grew louder: *"Does any of that matter?"* And then, with more force, *"Will you obey?"*

\- - -

The word *obedience* carries with it an almost sour taste in our modern culture, even though it's a word we've known our entire lives. We work under rules, regulations, laws, and directives starting as children in our homes, then at school, then later when we enter the workforce. As parents, we create rules for our children, knowing some of them will inevitably be broken. We abide (more or less) by the laws of our lands—except when we're speeding or texting while driving to church. We listen to doctors and coaches who want to keep us healthy, strong, and safe. We blindly follow the advice of experts and authors as they lead us into business and creative pursuits. And yet for some reason, we still arch our backs and cock our eyebrows when we hear or read the word *obey*.

It falls into the same category as *submit*, and many of us (women especially), if we are honest, don't like the idea of relinquishing power—to anyone. As times and culture have changed, we've found creative ways to skirt around the idea of obedience. We've created legal loopholes and blurred the line between right and wrong, because we don't like to be told to "submit" to someone else or to "obey" a rule that might not agree with our "authentic self." There is little room to tell someone not to do something anymore, for their rights could be infringed upon and we could find ourselves facing legal battles. This word *obey*, which used to be common in marriage ceremonies, is omitted, and neither is it something that parents expect of their children. Kids today are not told that their decisions or behaviors are "bad" because, if they were, they could be "damaged psychologically."

— — —

When I started my research on the word *hustle*, I knew I would have to spend time examining the other side of our equation; *obedience* would need to become a word that I understood better. And so I dove in.

The first thing worth mentioning is that the usage of *obedience* follows a far different trajectory than that of *hustle*. While *hustle* has been on the rise in recent years, the exact opposite is true for *obedience*. Similarly, the definition of *obedience* has not changed over time like that of *hustle*, as we saw in chapter 1.

Here is what I found when I went searching for definitions of *obey*:

- to comply with or follow the commands, restrictions, wishes, or instructions of [a person or a law]
- to submit [to an authority]
- to carry out (instructions or orders)
- to behave or act in accordance with [a general principle, natural law, etc.][51]

---

[51] Dictionary.com, s.v. "obey," http://www.dictionary.com/browse/obey?s=t.

After serious inspection of its meaning, I wondered why so many people struggle with this term. Admittedly, those with a law enforcement background would be quick to defend the idea of compliance and its necessity to ensure order, safety, and peace in the world. But they aren't the only fans. God is also very fond of this word.

You can find it in almost every book of the Bible—from Genesis to Revelation. It is present in the earliest Jewish traditions of the Old Testament as well as in the teachings of Jesus and the letters to the first-century church.

The most quoted sections of scripture in regard to obedience are the first five books of the Bible—the original laws and rules handed down by God, through Moses, to the Israelites. There were specific instructions for almost every part of their lives and corresponding promises for those who adhered to God's commands. The book of Deuteronomy, especially, is full of covenants such as this one: "You will be blessed if you obey the commands of the LORD your God that I am giving you today."[52]

Many Christians wrongfully read this verse, claiming a "blessed life" the moment they surrender their hearts to Jesus. They fail to take note of the two-letter word directly following the word *blessed*. It's the hook on which the blessing hangs—*if*. *If* you obey the commands of the Lord, *then* you will be blessed.

The blessing isn't contingent on whether or not God *can* bless or even *wants* to, nor is this a promise for an influential, affluent, and crisis-free life. God doesn't spell out what kind of blessing He'll shower on His people—He

---

[52] Deuteronomy 11:27 NLT

just guarantees that He will. We know that God is good[53] and that He wants to bless His kids,[54] just like an earthly father wants to care well for his children. The point of this verse is not the assumption of the blessing, but that the blessing is contingent on obedience—the will and action put toward following God's commands.

Obedience is both a choice and an act of faith. It doesn't require that we have all the answers or that we understand or even agree with the action requested. My children, for instance, don't always comprehend why I ask them to do things—which are good for them physically, mentally, emotionally, or spiritually—but I don't need their buy-in for what I'm requiring them to do. When I told my toddlers not to touch the hot stove or run across the street without me, I didn't ask them if they liked my directions. I presumed there would be commands they wouldn't like, but I'm the parent and they are the children. I am the one with the greater wisdom, understanding, and knowledge; their perspective is limited, and their desires are often rooted in what is most pleasing to them in the moment.

I've found that my relationship with God tends to work the same way. He doesn't require me to sign off on His ideas or commands or even to like them. God doesn't ask me first if I feel like obeying His directions, or how I feel about what it is He's asking me to do.

Like any child, I am guilty of ignoring some of God's directions and completing only those commands that seem easy or that I enjoy. And let's not forget the whining, tantrums, huffing, puffing, and eye-rolling that occur when

---

[53] 1 Chronicles 16:34

[54] Matthew 7:11

God asks me to do something out of my comfort zone.

Sometimes our exchanges sound something like this:

> *"Malinda, I need you to forgive that person."*
>
> Really, God? Are You kidding me? *(Sometimes a mild expletive is added here because I know God can read my mind anyway.)* Don't You remember what that person has done—how I've been hurt?
>
> *"Yes, Malinda, of course I remember."*
>
> But it's so hard. I don't know if I can.
>
> *"Yet others have forgiven you for much more."*
>
> *(Gulp!)* Lord, I don't know if it will really change how my heart feels about that person.
>
> *"You just take the first step and let Me worry about what happens in your heart."*

Maybe you've been in a similar position, where God has asked you to do something uncomfortable like forgiving someone for an offense or a judgment that hurt you. These internal battles are especially difficult *because* they are internal—if we choose not to follow God's prompting, no one will ever know. Of course, there are also the scenarios where He expects our outward actions to mirror the words we have spoken—where He expects us to put money where our mouths are, often literally. Perhaps you've had an experience similar to one I had a couple of years ago.

My time in TJ Maxx had almost come to an end. I'd left the house with a hope that spending a couple of hours wandering with a fancy coffee in hand would fill me up. I was exiting the store with my purchases when I caught his hopeless gaze. His face was young, just like the hands that weakly held the brown cardboard sign that was perched between the legs of his dirty jeans.

Immediately I looked away (I knew better than to make eye contact!). I struggled to locate my phone from the bottomless abyss of the purse I carried. When I couldn't find it, I decided to pretend to scan the rows of cars for my vehicle (which I was able to spot quickly—two rows over, third minivan in). As I walked toward the silver refuge of my Odyssey, I continued to feel his eyes—searching, waiting, hoping.

"Malinda, go back to the kid with the cardboard sign."

God, how can I be sure he'll use my money wisely?

"You can't."

But, Lord, my husband has worked so hard to provide for our family. . .

"Interesting. I thought I was your provider."

You are. It's just that he's a teenager, and I have my own kids to take care of now.

"That's right—he's just a kid. Wouldn't you want someone to help one of your daughters if they were sitting in his position? Am I not the One who takes care of all your needs? Go on, Malinda, turn around. Empty your wallet. Extend hope. Offer dignity. Smile. Be a blessing."

(Gulp! Again.)

＿ ＿ ＿

Our obedience is what God is after. But not as a result of oppression under a brutal dictator nor because we've been threatened or compelled with fear tactics. Rather, His posture is that of a Father eager to release His children and watch as they make good choices. He knows our lives will be better when we relinquish control; He longs for us to surrender our wills.

Obedience to God is our faith worked out in our everyday decisions. His desire is that our ears be open and eager to hear His voice as we move throughout our day, not just when we're sitting with our Bibles and coffee in the morning or when we're sitting in a pew at church. Our posture is not weakly submitting to someone who is abusive or controlling, but rather living with open hands and a surrendered heart—believing that God has the better vantage point, the greater wisdom, and that, like any good father, if He's asking us to do something, it's for our own good.

CHAPTER 11

Jesus: Obedience in the Flesh

All creation holds its breath, waiting for God's response to Jesus' plea. Every element feels the agony in His voice, even if "Your will be done" was the final line of His prayer. His posture is one of surrender. He knows the time has come. He is willingly yielding to His Father.

The gnarled olive branches ache to gather and comfort the Son who spoke them into existence. The rocks and the ground steady themselves under the weight of the All-Powerful One, and the grass and leaves turn away from the excruciating scene before them. Each element of creation bends low to the King in nervous anticipation of what is to come—for they have seen and heard stories of God's wrath poured out on man and earth before; His love and just nature are well known. The Father will make the right choice; He always does. Of this they are sure.

The delay is no more than an instant, yet it feels like an eternity. Jesus sighs, knowing the answer before He even finished asking. His simple prayer to the Father was, "Is there another way?" He knows there isn't; this is the plan. The same plan they had come up with together long ago. Jesus is aware that pain will be involved, but the anguish of the upcoming separation from His Father is beyond bearable. The salty trails dripping from His forehead are no longer sweat but blood[55]—*another foreshadowing of what is to come.*

The ground beneath Him is damp with the tears, sweat, and blood of the Author of Life. The same hands that spanned the universe are now receiving strength from an angel, dispatched to sustain God the Son, for everything else on this side of heaven can only listen and watch.

This is the plan. It's what has to happen. It is the only way. Although Jesus is God's Son, He is about to learn obedience through His suffering.[56] *As He stands in Gethsemane's garden, creation bows low—the King is about to lay down His life; darkness is coming.*

Throughout scripture we read stories of individuals who exhibit incredible courage right alongside their colossal mistakes and personality quirks. We see them stumble and fall, rise to what God has appointed them to do, and struggle with total obedience. These ordinary men and women were called out of obscurity into moments of faith and action. Their life lessons and character traits are worth emulating, to be sure. But only one Person's life was always exemplary. He never wavered, never doubted. He didn't argue back and forth with God about the plan. He didn't choose surrender in one moment and then walk in pride the next. His movements were always calculated, always selfless, always God-honoring. This Man's name: Jesus.

In the case of every other leader or king, prophet or

---

[55] Luke 22:44

[56] Hebrews 5:8

apostle, we see moments of extraordinary strength and honor paralleled with giant lapses in judgment. We read about their lack of integrity or the fear that almost overcame them.

Jesus, in comparison, was obedient even at times when His actions make no sense to our finite minds. For example, when He let Jairus's daughter die so that He could stop and speak with the bleeding woman.[57] As a parent, I read that story and ask the gut-wrenching question, "Why was that woman's health more important than the dying child?"

When we see Him mix dirt and saliva and smear the mud on the man's eyes,[58] we cringe and think, *Really, Jesus, was that necessary? You could have just said the word and the healing would have been instantaneous!* We see Him repeatedly extending grace to the men who would later abandon Him in His greatest hour of need,[59] and we roll our eyes with impatience. *Surely if we'd had the same opportunity—to walk in His footsteps—we never would have made the mistakes of Thomas, James, and poor old Peter.* Yeah, right!

We read about how He healed some people but not everyone and imagine the irritation that family members must have felt when it seemed that Jesus was never in a hurry. The Gospels repeatedly show Him making time for the outcasts, the forgotten, the broken, but not for the influencers of His day (the opposite emphasis of today's culture). We know that the parables Jesus told often stumped His audience and that He chose not to unleash His power when doing so literally could have saved His life.

---

[57] Luke 8:49, 43–48

[58] John 9:6

[59] Matthew 26:56

We read that Jesus never did anything without His Father's approval,[60] and we understand that God's ways and wisdom often look odd to our human perspective.[61] So we accept these details because we believe that Jesus knew something we didn't, and if He was obedient to His own death,[62] then surely in all other matters He was doing exactly what His Father had asked Him to do.

Jesus, the Son of God, remained faithful to God the Father. John records Jesus' words in chapter 5: "I tell you the truth, the Son can do nothing by himself. He does only what he sees the Father doing. Whatever the Father does, the Son also does."[63]

I have to admit that when the obedience of Jesus works for my benefit, it's easier to accept. If I'm talking about salvation, I have no problem partaking in His obedience, and I'm overwhelmed with gratitude. But when it comes to a child's health or to a young parent's life that hangs in the balance, or when disasters strike the most vulnerable, I tend to want to question God's methods, timing, and plan. That may sound contemptuous to you, but haven't we all struggled with the question, "Why has this bad thing happened to such a good person?"

Consider for a moment what Martha and Mary must have thought as they sent news to Jesus of Lazarus's sickness. Their sisterly dialogue may have sounded something like this:

---

[60] John 5:19

[61] Isaiah 55:8

[62] Hebrews 5:8

[63] John 5:19 NLT

Mary: "Let's send word to Jesus."

Martha: "Do you really think He'll come?"

Mary: "Of course He'll come; Lazarus is one of His dear friends."

Martha: "I'm afraid He won't get the message in time."

Mary: "He will, Martha."

Martha: "What if it's too late?"

Mary: "He will come, Martha. He won't let His friend die."

Perhaps this conversation is one you've had yourself. Maybe the pain of reflecting on it is excruciating because you're reading from a place of deep suffering or grief. You've sat in the hospital room or alone in the darkness as someone you dearly loved slipped from this life into the next. And your question that remains unanswered is, "Aren't You going to do something, Jesus?"

We beat our fists into the carpet or swing them in the air. *Why are the unborn being targeted? Why are the poor forgotten? Why do children suffer through cancer?* We don't believe that the bad things occurring in our broken and fallen world are God's fault, but we don't understand why He doesn't move on our behalf. We want to picture Him as One who is near to the brokenhearted. We long to believe that He sees our suffering and pain. We are eager to feel His presence, to hear His voice, to see His hand in our everyday lives. But we also struggle when He doesn't answer our prayers the way we want Him to.

It's hard to find peace in the midst of the silence, but it is impossible to ignore His quiet response. In these moments, when He leans in and cups our cheeks with a sweetness that can come only from One who has bled and died for us, He whispers, *"Oh, My child, I have done so much."*

The pain He endured, the humiliation of being separated from His Father, the time He was required to wait before fully unleashing the force of His power and authority over death—all of it was under the watchful, knowing, condoning gaze of His Father. God's plan set in motion thousands of years earlier was complete in the death, burial, and resurrection of His one and only Son. It was the Son's obedience that granted us access to God the Father—for our salvation, for our healing, for the power we need to endure our current struggles and heartaches. In one act of obedience, Jesus covered us, completely, from everything we would ever do and everything we would ever have to face.

Let's go back to the story of Jesus learning that His dear friend was sick.[64] Lazarus hadn't contracted a common cold or flu virus; he was literally on his deathbed. Let that thought sink in—what would it feel like if one of your closest friends was hospitalized in the next town over and was not expected to survive? In this scenario, what would you do if you had the power to pull your friend back from death's door? It's a difficult scene to digest, but the solution comes instantaneously—we would drop everything and go to our friend. There would be no hesitation, no pause for prayer. We would move swiftly. And yet, what did Jesus do?

He didn't move at all.[65]

---

[64] John 11:3 NLT

[65] John 11:6

He didn't jump on a donkey and trot off quickly. He didn't send someone on ahead of Him with the message that He was coming and not to panic. He didn't bow His head and offer a prayer. This is a perfect example of a time when Jesus could have and, in our minds, *should have* hustled to get something done, and yet He didn't. He waited two days. *(Imagine that for a moment. Surely additional messages would have been sent. Undoubtedly Peter called a meeting to discuss whether they should confront Jesus' lack of urgency.)* Jesus waited two days as Lazarus's body continued to deteriorate. Then, when Jesus finally decided it was time to go to the home of His friend (much at the urging of the disciples, no doubt), the journey to Bethany took days. When He arrived, His beloved friend had been dead four days.[66] Four days!

This would have been an almost unbearable trip for His traveling companions, and the longest days of Martha and Mary's lives. And perhaps you know too well what "waiting" does to the soul.

Maybe you're fortunate enough to have escaped the pain of a physical loss. You've never had to sit in a doctor's office and feel the air being sucked from the room. There hasn't been a whisper of suicide, cancer, or trauma that ripped someone you loved from your life, leaving you scarred and fumbling after your faith. But perhaps you've endured a different loss. Your pain is not from a physical loss but is emotional in nature. The hurt is an ache that never goes away. Every day you have sent word to Jesus, like Martha and Mary, asking Him to come quickly, to help you, to relieve you of the suffering, to move on your behalf.

---

[66] John 11:17

We want to have a baby and start our family, but the child God wants us to love won't be born for another five years.

We want to see a miraculous healing for the family member who is an addict, but God wants that person to learn self-discipline and self-care.

We want a financial blessing, but He wants us to learn stewardship with the little He's placed in our hands.

We want our business to take off or our kids to obey; we want a best friend's forgiveness or a father's love. We want our futures to unfold in the exact way we deem best.

And some of us want an audible voice to give us an answer to the questions that are on repeat—the ones that lull us to sleep at night and begin before we've even pulled our eyelids from their slumber: *Why didn't You come, Jesus? Why didn't You do anything when it was in Your power? Why didn't You move more quickly?*

Why, why, why?

And though you want to believe that Jesus hears you, sometimes you wonder. Because what does He do? It feels like nothing. It seems that He is staying put. He waits. The pain of His inaction is harder to swallow than the turmoil we are living in. Yet. . .who are we to question God?

Jesus didn't.

When He moved, it was because His Father said it was time. When He healed, it was because the Father told Him to. When He stayed away (as in the case of Lazarus), we have to trust that it was because God said, *"Wait."*

God is never early. He is never late. He isn't deaf to our cries, and He isn't capable of making mistakes. Lazarus died, and not every sick individual received instantaneous healing regardless of their proximity to Jesus. The lame man at Bethesda was healed, yet there were "crowds" waiting at the pool.[67] In Mark's Gospel we read, "Many sick and demon-possessed people were brought to Jesus," and He healed "many" of them—note it doesn't say He healed them all.[68] Jesus did only as He saw His Father doing.

In the case of Lazarus, He waited until there was death. Until there was no way out. No more hope for his family. Nothing left but to prepare the body for burial. Martha and Mary were no longer by his bedside, on their knees in prayer. They had abandoned all belief that their brother would be well again. And what did Jesus do? He spoke a command: "Lazarus, come out." And the dead man rose.

How many of our prayers does God answer when we impatiently demand Him to versus when He deems the time is right? How often does He wait to respond to our requests until the time when His power can best be revealed? I wonder how many of our dreams He plans to resurrect at the perfect time, perhaps after they are dead and forgotten. Is He simply waiting for us to surrender first—to stop trying to figure it out, come up with workable solutions, and solve all the problems ourselves?

Jesus' radical, continual, humble submission to the ways and will of His Father is the greatest example to us of what it means to fully obey. What would happen if, when we came to God with our list of requests, we simply opened our hands and prayed like Jesus did: "Not my will, but Yours be done"?[69]

---

[67] John 5:3

[68] Mark 1:32–34

[69] Luke 22:42

CHAPTER 12

Complete Obedience

"So where are we headed?" asks the man with a strong grip on the arm of his closest companion.

"The pool of Siloam," the blind man answers assuredly.

"Are you sure that's where Jesus told you to go?" the man questions with one eyebrow cocked as he glances around for confirmation from someone else that Siloam was indeed the correct destination.

"Yes, I am sure. He was specific." The blind man stops and turns his solemn face toward his friend.

"Why don't we try someplace closer? This pool over here—it's supposed to have healing powers, you know. Does it really matter which waters you get into? Jesus already put the mud on your eyes. Can't you just wash it off wherever you want?"

The blind man shrugs off the hand that he had trusted to lead him. His voice is confident and his words calculated as he tells his guide to take him to Siloam without further delay or skeptical remarks. The man sighs but trudges forward, happy his friend can't see his doubting expression. The blind man walks on, resolute in his decision to follow Jesus' directions, as peculiar as they may be.

Throughout the Bible we find countless stories of God at work in the details. When Naaman was told to wash in the

Jordan seven times, he received a specific place and an exact number of plunges. Joshua was given explicit directions for marching around the city of Jericho—the number of laps to be completed in total silence, with the priests leading the charge. The Israelites couldn't collect more than a day's worth of manna, Gideon was required to send away most of his army, Noah was to complete the ark to precise specifications, and the disciples became empowered only after waiting for the Holy Spirit to come upon them in Jerusalem.

To say that God cares about the details is a gross understatement. His awareness of the very number of hairs on each of our heads is just a sample of His knowledge of us.[70] He knows the longings of our hearts, our dreams for the future, the fears that keep us awake at night, and the purposes that propel us forward. He gives His instructions not out of OCD but out of loving concern for our own good. In the process of showing us how to surrender, God draws us closer to His heart, which is His ultimate goal.

The Gospel of John includes the story of Jesus using mud to heal someone. Not an army general, a king, or the son of an influential leader. This man goes unnamed in the Gospels; he is defined only by his disability. And the mud Jesus used for the miracle, it wasn't a particular type of clay, like the kind used in spas and high-end skin-care lines. It had a simple formula: one part dirt from the ground mixed with one part holy saliva.

[Jesus] spit on the ground, made mud with the saliva,

---

[70] Luke 12:7

*and spread the mud over the blind man's eyes. He told
him, "Go wash yourself in the pool of Siloam" (Siloam
means "sent"). So the man went and washed and came
back seeing!*[71]

Before we continue, it's interesting to note that the blind
man did *not* receive his sight the moment Jesus' hands
made contact with his body. The Gospels record many
accounts of when a simple touch of His hand brought
instantaneous healing. In others, miracles ensued the
moment He spoke the words with authority. In this account, however, the blind man's healing was delayed. The
story continues:

*His neighbors and others who knew him as a blind
beggar asked each other, "Isn't this the man who used
to sit and beg?" Some said he was, and others said,
"No, he just looks like him!"*
    *But the beggar kept saying, "Yes, I am the same one!"
They asked, "Who healed you? What happened?"*
    *He told them, "The man they call Jesus made mud
and spread it over my eyes and told me, 'Go to the pool
of Siloam and wash yourself.' So I went and washed,
and now I can see!"*[72]

For a minute, let's assume that the blind man couldn't get
to this specific pool alone. We don't know how far away
Siloam was from his encounter with Jesus or what the
journey was like for him. It's safe to say that the blind

---

[71] John 9:6–7 NLT

[72] John 9:8–11 NLT

man probably required some assistance along the way. So either a friend had been standing near him and, having heard Jesus' directives, offered help, or the blind man somehow managed to recruit a helper to guide him on his quest.

Picture it how you will, but there's a good chance the blind man had to resist the urge to wipe his face clean the first chance he had. Perhaps he did as so many of us would have and questioned whether Jesus made a mistake in the directions given. Maybe he thought to himself, *Surely there must be another pool, another location, another way.* Maybe the blind man had heard this sort of promise before, *"Do this and be healed,"* only to return home still shrouded in darkness. We don't know if he moved quickly or considered forgetting about his encounter with Jesus altogether. Regardless of any doubts and fears he may have had, we know he chose to move forward in the direction Jesus told him to go.

But what if he hadn't? What if he'd let the human thoughts derail him? *It was an odd set of instructions after all.* How many of us have allowed the plan to be forgotten because we questioned whether we could have misinterpreted what we thought we heard Him say?

Tell me if this sounds familiar: You have a meaningful encounter with God during which He whispers something specific to your heart—an idea regarding a problematic child, a distant spouse, or a demanding boss. But instead of obeying His instructions, you "wipe the mud from your eyes" and move forward with your own plan. Even though God was clear, you reach for the latest self-help book and gather friends for a prayer meeting on the matter. You sign up for an expensive diet plan, even though He told you to work on the discipline of eating healthy and walking every day. You pay for another month of counseling sessions, even though He asked you to forgive and go back to your spouse. You've been struggling to grow your business or expand your platform, thinking that when you arrive "there," you'll be better positioned to carry out His plan, but you fail to see that He has given you influence and opportunity right now (it just may not look the way you want it to look).

In all these scenarios, we are like the blind man, having received the remedy for our problem. But rather than following Jesus' directions and completing the process of our healing, we move forward with our own plans.

What would have happened to the blind man had he not followed Jesus' directions? What if he had waited overnight, with the hope that soaking in the mud would make the healing more complete? Would his sight have been restored had he washed someplace else or allowed a friend to bring him water from the pool instead of walking there himself and washing as instructed? I don't think so. It was when he obeyed every part of Jesus' directions that he received his miracle. *The man's obedience activated the miracle.*

Don't miss that.

Jesus extended mercy and healing power. He concocted the recipe and gave it freely to the man. But the key to experiencing the miracle was when the man applied his faith *and then* walked in obedience. Sometimes we think it's enough to have great faith. And to be fair, that is an excellent place to start. But as much as the blind man *believed* in the power that Jesus possessed, the healing power was not transferred until he made the journey to the pool of Siloam. And once he was there, he was still blind. The miracle occurred as he put his faith to action. When he chose to plunge into the pool, his eyes were turned on by the hand of God. The blind man had to do the physical work of getting to the right place. He had to wash. His *act* of obedience released his miracle.

How many of us are sitting comfortably, believing from afar that Jesus is who He said He was and that His power is available to us, and yet we are unable to receive a breakthrough because we choose to remain still? How many times has the miracle been aborted because of our failure or refusal to get in the game and meld our faith and our obedience? How many times have we fallen short of obtaining the Lord's provision because we obeyed part of the instruction but not all of it?

- - -

Let's look at another story from a different time in history, when God gave specific directions to someone, but instead of following them to the letter, this person decided to comply with only some of the details. He believed his wisdom was higher than God's, and it cost him much.

The man in the story is King Saul from the Old Testament—the very first king of the Israelites. He must have been quite a man for God to have chosen him as the prototype in a new kind of leadership structure. Here's what we know about Saul:

> *There was a man of [the tribe of] Benjamin whose name was Kish. . .a mighty man of valor. He had a son whose name was Saul, a choice and handsome*

man, and there was not a more handsome person than
he among the sons of Israel; from his shoulders and up
he was [a head] taller than any of the people."[73]

So Saul's dad was influential and wealthy, and Saul was tall and handsome. Not exactly a long list of strong character traits. I guess that's why God did a rewiring of his heart[74]—enough that people took notice of how different he was.[75] He was the man people wanted to see, and God changed his heart so that he could lead the people well as a king.

Over time, however, Saul's heart changed again; it was no longer eager to follow God. When Saul was commissioned to destroy the Amalekites, the message from God was specific, leaving no room for creative license. Unfortunately, because he didn't follow all of the instructions, Saul lost the throne:

> *Samuel said, "There was a time when you didn't think*
> *you were important. But you became the leader of the*
> *tribes of Israel. The LORD anointed you to be king over*
> *Israel. He sent you to do something for him. He said,*
> *'Go and completely destroy the Amalekites. Go and*
> *destroy those evil people. Fight against them until you*
> *have wiped them out.' Why didn't you obey the LORD?*
> *Why did you keep for yourselves what you had taken*
> *from your enemies? Why did you do what is evil in*
> *the sight of the LORD?"*
>
> *"But I did obey the LORD," Saul said.*

---

[73] 1 Samuel 9:1–2 NASB

[74] 1 Samuel 10:9

[75] 1 Samuel 10:11–12

[Side note: "But" is probably not the best way to begin a response to God. It puts you on the defense, which means you're feeling guilty. Saul didn't get this memo. He continues:]

"I went to do what he sent me to do. I completely destroyed the Amalekites. I brought back Agag, their king. The soldiers took sheep and cattle from what had been taken from our enemies. They took the best of what had been set apart to God. They wanted to sacrifice them to the LORD your God at Gilgal."

But Samuel replied, "What pleases the LORD more? Burnt offerings and sacrifices, or obeying the LORD? It is better to obey than to offer a sacrifice. . . ."

"You have refused to do what the LORD told you to do. So he has refused to have you as king over Israel! . . . The LORD has torn the kingdom of Israel away from you today. He has given it to one of your neighbors. He has given it to someone better than you."[76]

This may seem like a harsh punishment—stripping a man of his throne when what was held back was given to God as a sacrifice! Saul and his soldiers did offer the animals to the Lord, but that was not what God had wanted. Saul's decision showed that he thought he was wiser than God. It's the echo from the garden all over again, the belief that what we are doing is *what God really wants*. It's the same lie—that our wisdom is better than God's. Perhaps now you're starting to understand how much God desires obedient hearts.

---

[76] 1 Samuel 15:17–22, 26, 28 NIRV

He doesn't desire hearts that say yes but then don't follow through; He desires hearts that obey totally. Not partially, apathetically agreeing to what God commands, but fully surrendered and eager to do whatever it is He has asked.

If God has asked you to start a business or write a book, move forward and stop stalling in the "research" phase you've been parked in for the last year. If God has told you to forgive someone, forgive and move on without holding past mistakes over that person as a weapon when it suits you. He may have called you to help the homeless where you live, and you've been spending a fortune driving downtown to do so when what He really wants you to do is to uproot your family from your comfy four-bedroom-three-car-garage home with a sprawling backyard in the burbs and make the geographical move into the city. He wants you to fully embrace the thing He's asked you to do.

Just as parents expect their children to obey when they're given a set of instructions, God wants us to follow His guidance. We don't get to decide which commands are for us or whether God's wisdom is the best choice. Followers of Jesus are those who willingly surrender their own plans and obey completely.

CHAPTER 13

Obedient When the Dream Isn't Yours

*"What's an ark, Lord?" Noah asks, scratching his head.
"And while we're talking, what exactly do You mean
when You say 'floodwaters'?" He looks toward heaven
and runs his hand through his hair, confused because of
the cloudless sky. "I mean, I know we're on good terms,
but this is a whole new level, Lord. Are You sure I'm
the one You want to take on such an enormous task?
I'm a farmer, after all, not a skilled woodworker."*

*There is a pause. He shifts his weight anxiously,
waiting for God to return his arguments with con-
cession. But the silence hangs thick, and finally he
blurts out, "Okay, Lord, I'll do it. Why not? Even if I
don't know how this whole thing is going to pan out,
or how to gather all these animals, or how to collect
enough food to feed them, I'll do it because You asked
me. Not because I think I can or because I'm confident
that it will work. But because You asked me, I'll do it."*

There will be times throughout our lives when getting
excited about an idea is easy. We have a dream or someone gives a great talk at church or a conference, and we're
left scribbling wildly and churning the plans over in our
minds for days. Sometimes the inspiration comes from the
most random places in the most unusual ways, but regardless, it is something we can get behind. We are not just

eager but ecstatic about pursuing the vision that we believe is God-ordained—especially if it's something we know others will be excited about too.

But what happens when that God-dream isn't a trendy idea or when pursuing His plan will probably leave us a few followers short with a couple of friends who have turned their backs to us? Will we still go after that dream excitedly, or will we let it pass us by because it doesn't fit into our five-year plan, personal brand, season of life, or budget?

What would we do if God handed us a plan that seemed so out of left field that we questioned our ability to discern His voice from the others? What if the thing He asked us to do is not just beyond our ability or means but actually sounds a little crazy? For me, it sounded like, *"Quit your job that contributes 30 percent of your family's income, even though you've just increased your monthly expenses by 30 percent."* I remember being so sure that what I was stepping into was God's plan, even though it was terrifying. I knew I was in good company, though, because others had gone before me, and their orders had sounded even crazier. At least I wasn't asked to "march around a fortified city in silence," "attack the enemy's camp with torches and horns," or my personal favorite, "build a giant boat in your front yard."

When we step out into the land of crazy, God-sized plans, no one can offer more sympathy than a man named Noah. Yes, Noah-and-the-ark Noah. The one who remained after God decided to rid the world of all humanity and start fresh.[77]

---

[77] Genesis 6:13

The Bible describes the world of Noah's day as full of corruption and violence.[78] Yet in the midst of the darkness and despair, a single ray of hope emerged: his name was Noah. One day God struck up a conversation with him and shared His plan for the future: Earth 2.0, which happened to include Noah and his family. Now, for a moment I want you to consider what that exchange might have felt like for Noah. We don't get the insider's look at what thoughts were racing through his mind or how high his blood pressure rose. We don't know if he processed through the gamut of emotions (like most of us do) or whether he chose humility, honored that God would assign him to such a monumental task.

Have you ever stopped to wonder what would have happened if Noah had responded differently—if he had walked away when God presented the plan, or if, after working countless years, he decided it wasn't worth it and chose to leave the half-constructed ark and forge his own destiny? What if Noah had balked when God handed out his job, reacting the way we tend to when God hands us a task to complete: "Me, God—are You kidding? I'm way overqualified to do manual labor." Or maybe we don't take the high road but wallow in self-deprecation: "God, that is such a large assignment; I don't have near enough experience or influence. Maybe You should ask someone else to do this—they'd probably do a better job anyway."

Unfortunately for Noah, he was the only option—the

---

[78] Genesis 6:11

one person who had a relationship with God.[79] So whether Noah ran his mouth—giving God a list of reasons he couldn't or shouldn't be the one to complete the mission—or silently went about completing the task, we know one thing: Noah did the work.

He didn't start off with enthusiasm only to abandon his work later. Scripture says that "Noah did everything just as God commanded him."[80] *Everything.* Not part of the task, but all of it. And there were a lot of details!

> *"Build a large boat from cypress wood and waterproof it with tar, inside and out. Then construct decks and stalls throughout its interior. Make the boat 450 feet long, 75 feet wide, and 45 feet high. Leave an 18-inch opening below the roof all the way around the boat. Put the door on the side, and build three decks inside the boat—lower, middle, and upper."*[81]

God didn't exactly give Noah creative freedom for this project—His instructions were specific. Not only for the actual construction of the boat, but for all that Noah was to collect and bring with him as well:

> *"You are to bring into the ark two of all living creatures, male and female, to keep them alive with you. Two of every kind of bird, of every kind of animal and of every kind of creature that moves along the ground will come to you to be kept alive. You are to*

---

[79] Genesis 6:8

[80] Genesis 6:22 NIV

[81] Genesis 6:14–16 NLT

*take every kind of food that is to be eaten and store it
away as food for you and for them.*"[82]

In His infinite wisdom, God chose one man with a desire
to obey to carry out this vital task. He didn't send an army
general to conquer or a politician to rule. God planned to
use the sweat of a man's brow and the strength of his faith
to save from extinction all the animals on Earth and the
very people He had lovingly created. He didn't start over
with a new garden and Adam and Eve—He chose Noah.
God whispered His plan to Noah, who was five hundred
years old, giving him specific instructions to obey. And the
Bible tells us that he did.

Noah obeyed even when it didn't make sense, even
when he couldn't see what would eventually take shape.
Without knowing how long the rain would last, how many
days would pass before he'd see land again, or where they
would end up, Noah went into the ark with his family and
a zoo. And God.

What else was there to do? For a lot of us, there would
have been time to panic.

The delay between when Noah walked up the ramp
next to the giraffes and when the boat actually floated away
was significant. We tend to hear the story and think, *God
shut the door, and then it started raining,* but in reality, something different happened. Noah's family took refuge down
in the belly of the boat for seven days before God opened
the heavens.[83]

That would have been enough time for doubt to

---

[82] Genesis 6:19–21 NIV

[83] Genesis 7:1, 10

descend and take up residence in Noah's mind. It would have been more than enough time for the rest of his family to start arguing and grumbling about the stench of the animals, the cramped quarters, and whose turn it was to clean the stalls and feed the sheep. A week is a long time when we are waiting with anticipation for something epic to happen; and in Noah's case, he was certainly on (an apocalyptic) edge. Most of us probably would have built an escape hatch for moments like these or could have been found curled up in the fetal position in a dark corner, having succumbed to fear.

Why exactly did God wait? The Bible isn't clear about the purpose of the seven-day waiting period, but we do know that when it was over, everything changed. God brought the rains. The flood covered the earth, and Noah lost everything he'd ever known; he was literally face-to-face with the hand of God. I'm sure there were moments when Noah was perplexed at how and why he was the one sitting on the ark. He never could have imagined that building a floating zoo would be the thing people would remember him for—forever. It didn't make any sense.

But that is often how the story unfolds with God. The math doesn't make sense, but it still adds up. One barren wife and one old man become the promised parents of God's chosen people.[84] One young boy sold into slavery saves nations from starvation.[85] One Hebrew baby spared at birth leads two million people through the Red Sea on dry ground.[86] One eyeless man, with hands on the temple

---

[84] Genesis 18:11

[85] Genesis 37:28; 41:57

[86] Exodus 1:17; 14:21–22

pillars, kills the enemy leadership.[87] One prophet prays, and a drought ravages the land for three and a half years; then he prays again, and the rains come.[88]

This is what happens when we choose to obey—even when it doesn't make sense. When the odds are against us and we aren't sure whether to believe the naysayers or trust God at His word. I pray that in those moments we will be people who push forward in faith. I'm not advocating carelessness or negligence, but I am suggesting that our human wisdom can only take us so far, and that the steps beyond are those of pure faith. And obedience.

It was obedience that saved Noah and his family. Yes, the hand of God spared them, but the truth is, God didn't take away Noah's free will—the choice of whether to trust God and go along with the plan or to walk away and pursue his own path was his. The building of the ark was not Noah's brainchild. He probably didn't grow up as a young boy thinking that one day he'd be the head of the sole surviving family. The dream to sail around the flooded earth wasn't his—it was God's. And the plan probably didn't make sense at first, but he did it anyway.

What has God asked you to do?

Maybe it's ark-sized, but perhaps not. Maybe you feel that it is enormous, and you feel too small to tackle it. Perhaps it's a plan that was never on your radar, such as adopting a child later in life with children in high school or already moved out of the house, like several people I know. Maybe you're like my friend who has recently felt that God is asking her to move her family overseas for a season, even

[87] Judges 16:29–30

[88] James 5:17–18

though her life feels steady just the way it is right now. Perhaps God is asking you to give up the dream job you've spent the last five years working hard toward because He has a new project or business He wants you to start. For others, this ask might be a call outside of your comfort zone to write a book, teach a class, start homeschooling, or speak at a retreat. (I can appreciate if you're feeling apprehensive about anything on this list!)

Whatever it is, whether it seems daunting or demeaning, may we have the heart of Noah to say, "Yes, Lord," even if it doesn't make sense. May we be those who can say, "I did everything the Lord told me to do," just as it was said about Noah.[89]

---

[89] Genesis 7:5 ERV

CHAPTER 14

Attitude Is Everything

"Who does he think he is?!" Naaman screams.

In horror, his servants watch as he curses loudly, and dust clouds fly in all directions from the force of his stomping. Silence fills the air as the chariot drivers exchange glances. They know they could be sitting for a while until their master's rage has calmed. Some decide to get comfortable in the shade; others roll their eyes in obvious embarrassment over this grown man's temper tantrum. Imagine, an army general carrying on like a child!

We tend to react like Naaman when we don't like the answer we've been given. Parents experience the tantrums of toddlers and teenagers, bosses get their fair share of attitude from employees, and God tends to get the worst of it—not only the fiery responses, but the smoldering anger of our hearts and hidden thoughts. I admit, I am still learning how to think first and react later. Those of us who are in the gut triad of the Enneagram[90] are especially prone to this type of behavior. Thankfully, I have several people who help me "off the edge" when I receive direction that I'd much rather ignore than comply with. Luckily for Naaman, he did also.

---

[90] See the Enneagram Institute website, https://www.enneagraminstitute.com/.

A few men nod to one another and slowly move to convene a short distance away. No one pays attention to the side discussion taking place—their voices are hushed and their faces expressionless. For all anyone knew, they could have been talking about what to prepare for the midday meal.

But suddenly their small assembly dashes off. Their pace is desperate; they are not fleeing but in pursuit. Within a minute they are breathless, having caught up with their master, Naaman. They know the protocol; they understand there will be a price for confronting their boss—for challenging the general. But it must be done. He turns around abruptly, aware of their presence. The men stand at attention, curious as to how he will respond. Each man holds his breath as the general's gaze moves from one face to another.

His eyes are red, not from a flash of rage, but from agony. They note the trails down his dusty cheeks and exhale silently, understanding that his anger has turned into frightened despair. They know how long he has carried his illness—the anxiety it has caused, the many fruitless attempts he has made to attain healing. And now, this final quest seems futile as well.

Finally, one man steps forward with extreme boldness and shares the collective feelings of the group. His voice is calm and sure, and the rest of the men gather closer around their master with empathy and a chorus of encouragement. "Why not do what the prophet said?" he pleads.

Naaman's eyes close and his head hangs; the posture of surrender is not one he chooses often, nor have any of his servants ever seen him concede. They each hold their breath and awkwardly scratch their faces to hide their smiles. While there is no guarantee, they inwardly cheer, even as their outer demeanor remains solemn. For now, they have convinced this powerful man to obey someone else's command. They return to their chariots with a new mission—they are headed to the Jordan River, and maybe Naaman will yet receive healing.

— — —

The short story of Naaman in 2 Kings is full of powerful lessons, and I've returned to it over and over in my life. It is the account of an army general afflicted with a disease and the way he received his healing. Until recently, I thought that the story of Naaman receiving his miracle was a story of obedience. He was told where to go and what to do, and when he followed the directives to the letter, his body was restored. But that's not the whole story. As I was studying the entire account, I realized that Naaman's obedience was not immediate, and his attitude was less than stellar.

Naaman was a typical army general—accustomed to getting his way in almost all things. He was eager to be done with this disease and was probably used to influencing others to give him what he wanted. Perhaps it could be said that Naaman was a hustler. That's why, instead of humbly going to the prophet he had been told to see, he packed up a caravan full of gifts and appeared to the king of Israel with the expectation of buying his healing.

"Well then, go," said the king of Aram. "And I'll send a letter of introduction to the king of Israel."

So he went off, taking with him about 750 pounds of silver, 150 pounds of gold, and ten sets of clothes.

Naaman delivered the letter to the king of Israel. The letter read, "When you get this letter, you'll know that I've personally sent my servant Naaman to you; heal him of his skin disease."

When the king of Israel read the letter, he was terribly upset, ripping his robe to pieces. He said, "Am I a god with the power to bring death or life that I get orders to heal this man from his disease? What's going on here? That king's trying to pick a fight, that's what!"[91]

Soon after the king's outburst, Elisha received word about the strange request and sent the king a message with instructions for Naaman to come to his home.[92] So Naaman left the king and went to meet with the prophet, only to be further insulted when Elisha sent a servant with a message instead of greeting him personally.[93]

But the directions were specific: Naaman was told where to travel to and precisely how to bathe in order to be cleansed of his leprosy. Instead of reacting with gratitude or quickly executing the simple set of instructions, Naaman pitched a fit and stomped off. Most translations of verse 12 describe his mood as "a rage."

If it weren't for what happened next, Naaman never would have received his miracle:

---

[91] 2 Kings 5:5–7 MSG

[92] 2 Kings 5:8

[93] 2 Kings 5:10

But his servants caught up with him and said,
"Father, if the prophet had asked you to do something
hard and heroic, wouldn't you have done it? So why
not this simple 'wash and be clean'?"[94]

Naaman had gone to Elisha with an expectation of how he wanted to be healed. It included fanfare—a grand reception—yet in reality he was told he'd have to do something to be cleansed of his illness. It wasn't grueling work; he didn't have to offer a sacrifice (except maybe his pride), which was a common practice in Jewish culture to be rid of impurities. Also customary was to appear before a priest, recite prayers, and render payment for healing, but none of these commands were given to Naaman. The instructions were simple, yet what he wanted was to be asked to do something "great" (NIV).

As I read this verse, I felt a nudge to my ribs and a whisper to my heart, *"Isn't that most people?"*

I believe many of us want God to ask us to do the "hard and heroic" things, the "great" things, and the "difficult" things; but when God responds with simple instructions, we storm off in a huff—just like Naaman.

Maybe we aren't coming to Him with a request for healing but for something else significant, and God responds with a practical command just the same. We want to be debt-free; He tells us to give, to budget, to get a second job. We want to experience authentic community, and the whisper is, *"Make the phone call, open your doors, choose vulnerability."* We want to have greater influence

[94] 2 Kings 5:13 MSG

and inspire the masses, and He points us to our church, our next-door neighbor, or (gulp) our children, and says, *"Start there."* Nothing grand, just simple instructions carried out in anonymous ways.

How many times have we reacted like Naaman and stomped off in rage because God didn't respond to us the way we wanted? He asked us to do something simple, but our pride almost caused us to miss getting our miracle.

Fortunately, Naaman did obey eventually. He was blessed to have God-fearing servants with equal parts humility and courage. Verse 13 is the climax of Naaman's life. Without it, the story would be over. Listening to his servants was Naaman's first step toward humility. As is often the case, the physical healing was only part of the miracle. God didn't just want to restore Naaman's physical body; He planned to rewire Naaman's heart also.

Our culture of entitlement tells us that we can *have it all.* We demand our way, on our timeline, and we assert our right to customize every part of our lives. And if others fall short of our expectations, we dismiss them and throw a three-year-old's tantrum on the floor.

Naaman could have gone to another river, washed seven times, and remained afflicted. He could have plunged into the Jordan six times and not received his healing. He could have asked his servants to draw the water out and bathe him—and still stayed leprous. Why? Because the miracle wasn't in the water. Naaman wasn't cured because of how many times he immersed himself or how hard he scoured his skin—the breakthrough came when he chose to humble his heart. Once his attitude had changed, his healing was released.

After hearing the wisdom from his servants, Naaman finally listened. He *traveled to* the Jordan. He *got into* the water. He *washed*—not once, but *seven times*, as ordered by the prophet. He obeyed fully, and he was healed instantly.

Reading this account with fresh eyes made me wonder how often we miss the answer to our prayers, the freedom we seek, the favor we desire because our hearts are hard. We heard the instructions, but they didn't come in the way we expected or didn't feel the way we wanted, and so we didn't obey. We wanted God to ask us to do something "great," something "difficult," something "heroic," and instead we heard the opposite:

"Stay at home."
"Keep working at your day job."
"Close the business."
"Embrace motherhood."
"Grow slowly."
"Pay off your debt."
"Forgive that person."
"Love the least."
"Serve your local church/leaders."
"Love your neighbors."
"Be anonymous."
"Walk in humility."

Obedience is often difficult because it isn't the shiny and sexy stuff of faith. We won't get external praise and recognition for the things done in private—never mind the posture of our hearts. Obedience isn't typically Instagram worthy—especially if God has told you to give it up—and it requires that we check our attitudes often. Naaman received his healing only when he humbly obeyed and completed every step of the instructions Elisha had laid out. It was an all-or-nothing offer. And I can't help but wonder what would happen if we too did what God asked us to do—regardless of how simple the instructions. Would we see our prayers answered, our breakthroughs take place, our miracles happen before our eyes? How often do we miss out on what God is doing because our attitudes need an adjustment?

CHAPTER 15

Obedience Equals Maturity

When people asked me how I felt about quitting my day job, I described it as what I figured standing on top of a cliff in a base-jumping squirrel suit might feel like—toes hugging the edge of the rock with a breeze on my face. I knew God had asked me to trust Him, even if it didn't make sense, even if I was scared, even if no one else understood. When I surrendered, the peace overwhelmed me. I knew that jumping would result in a free fall at first—that was the terrifying part. But I held on to the belief that the wind would eventually get caught in the suit I was wearing and within seconds I would soar. Still, I had to jump. God was not going to push me off the cliff; I had to be the one to make a move, to step out in faith—to choose obedience.

People told me I was crazy. They commented that they "could never do something crazy like quitting a day job without already having a backup plan in place." And the idea that I circled back to, over and over, is that jumping with God is a lot like learning to skydive (well, from what I've learned through research anyway).[95]

When God asks us to jump, He typically doesn't start with something as large as giving up a job, moving to a foreign country, or giving away half our salary. For most

---

[95] As a side note, my best friend told me we should go skydiving once this book is published. I'm not sure if I have the guts to jump from a perfectly operational plane, so we'll have to see what happens.

people, His voice isn't a clap of thunder that wakes us one night demanding we start a company, marry someone, or walk away from the business we've spent years developing. Sometimes God works that way, but for most of us, He eases us in—just as you learn the basics before you go sky-diving for the first time.

You don't leap out of a plane without any prior training or support. You begin by jumping with someone—a trained instructor who has completed hundreds of jumps. Actually, you begin with on-the-ground training that doesn't require a plane at all. Once you've been cleared to jump, you go up in a plane with someone right next to you. You aren't kicked from the doorway; no one forces you to leap. You fall out the door with your instructor attached to you. If something goes wrong, you have the security of knowing that someone with greater knowledge and experience is there to help. You're not alone. Once you have completed the appropriate amount of training and jumps, you graduate to jumping solo.[96] You are able to free-fall from higher because you know not only what to expect, but how to react. The same is true in our faith journeys with God.

God's way of maturing our relationship with Him is by incrementally moving us toward places of greater obedience. Each step requires a little more faith to be exerted on our part. Like the person who begins by giving a 10 percent income tithe, each year deciding to give away a fraction more until one day they are living on less than half of their salary. Or the person who starts befriending neighbors and, over time, welcomes an exchange student,

---

[96] See the website for the United States Parachute Association: http://uspa.org/.

then a foster child, then a homeless woman, only to realize one day that the kitchen table is full of people in need.

God refines us through simple instructions and invitations to obey Him. He presses our hearts and challenges our motives; He asks us to open our hearts, our wallets, and our doors wider. He continues to require something greater of us because He knows He can.

— — —

As a parent, I do a disservice to my children if I expect too much from them for their age and maturity level. I do not assume that my six-year-old and eight-year-old will behave the same way. As they grow older, my hope is that I will be able to entrust them with more responsibility. I also eagerly anticipate more mature decisions as they develop and expect greater levels of communication with them. My desire is that they will have a complete understanding of the rules and directions given to them, not just by me but by God. The longer I parent, the more I come to understand my relationship with God the same way.

He is my Father, and His desire is for me to grow and mature in all areas of my life, including my ability to know His voice and respond when He speaks. My relationship with Him and my heart are what He's most concerned with, and these can only grow over time and with sacrifice. I know He's not going to ask me to do anything He won't also walk with me through or equip me for—even if it feels terrifying. His still, small voice has become more discernible the longer I've walked with Him, and as my faith has grown stronger, He has been able to ask me to take more sizable risks.

Our faith muscles—the ability to trust God's voice

no matter what He's asking and to move forward with courage—take time to develop. They require continual movement in the direction He's leading us and a stripping of ourselves along the way. It's often painful, the pruning, and it can be challenging to see the growth until someone else brings it to our attention (whether they realize they are doing so or not).

The casual comments sound like, "I could *never* do what you're doing," or similarly, "I love the way God speaks to you." These words have not always come from a place of encouragement but rather disbelief (or relief) on the part of the speaker. Yet it's in the midst of such conversations that I am reminded of how much my faith has grown.

When I first started walking with Jesus, I didn't have faith to quit my job. Or to give sacrificially. Or to share about my faith the way I do now. I didn't know that God delighted in setting goals with me such as, *"How much money will you give away this next year?"* or *"Who are you going to befriend/disciple?"* or that He's eager for my questions such as, "What's next, God?" These moments of clarity are so appreciated, because truthfully, there seem to be more moments when I am painfully aware of how those faith muscles have grown: gradually, and with much exercise.

— — —

I love how Eugene Peterson phrased 1 Thessalonians 5:12 in *The Message*: "And now, friends, we ask you to honor those leaders who work so hard for you, who have been given the responsibility of urging and guiding you along in your obedience." I remember reading this verse, which I had read many times before, and suddenly having the word *obedience* seared into my heart. It was the weight Peterson placed not only on the leaders mentioned and their responsibilities (as I had previously heard emphasized) but on individual believers too. It was no longer just another verse telling me to honor my spiritual leaders (which is a serious responsibility, no doubt), but it was now a reminder that I was to be *moving along* in my spiritual walk. The role of pastors and mentors is to urge me along, not entertain or coddle me. My journey was never meant to be a stationary one. And the only way to move from one place to the next is through obedience—saying yes to one question, taking one step in the direction God is leading, making one sacrifice at a time. Over time, these simple steps cause my faith to grow.

When physical muscles are nourished and conditioned, they become more flexible and substantial. But the care for them must be continual and intentional. You never grow stronger as a result of a part-time commitment to healthy eating and an active lifestyle. We don't become bodybuilders by watching videos, praying, and speaking in faith over our muscles. No, we have to act. We have to engage our bodies, not just our minds. And our spiritual muscles are no different.

Most of us would agree that actions must accompany our faith. We want Christians to "walk the walk, not just talk the talk." We believe that movement is necessary. James said it more bluntly in his book when he addressed the idea of faith without works: "In the same way, faith by itself, if it is not accompanied by action, is dead. But someone will say, 'You have faith; I have deeds.' Show me your faith without deeds, and I will show you my faith by my deeds."[97]

Almost all of us have heard some version of these words, if not quoted some portion of this message from James 2. We believe our outward actions must give credit to our words and beliefs—that faith by itself is dead. Faith muscles are not supposed to be insignificant; they are to be proved by our "deeds." And I would suggest that obedience is a necessary part of that equation.

It is obedience that moves us from one point in our faith to the next—not a mere feeling or a belief. Obedience is active participation, not just a nod of acknowledgment. It is continuous; it is the progression of our faith from fragile and helpless to courageous and tenacious. Obedience is choosing to let God lead and falling in behind Him with humility, not passivity. Obedience is faith in action, and the result is a maturity that can come only as we move in the direction He's asked—repeatedly.

Obedience is what James refers to as "deeds." It's the outcome of giving ourselves to Jesus fully and saying yes to whatever He's asking us to do. Yes to the physical actions of sharing our faith with our colleagues. Yes to starting a home Bible study. Yes to adopting a child. Yes to starting a blog, giving away a larger percentage of our income, or rolling up our sleeves and serving the homeless in our cities. For some, it's more heart and mind action that's required: dealing with fear and shame, going to therapy, or getting serious about kicking the addiction that no one knows about. Obedience is faith in action. It's turning our

[97] James 2:17–18 NIV

ears toward God's voice and moving in the direction He is pointing. Obedience is what matures our faith. Without it, our faith grows weak. It is immature, unyielding, selfish, stagnant, and powerless. James would even say "dead."

CHAPTER 16

Obedience When the Path Is Unclear

*D*anielle reached for another tissue in between the sobs that lurched her body forward and back. The whites of her eyes were bloodshot, her cheeks a mess of smudged mascara. When she looked across the table at me, it was with a piercing stare that left my heart racing. It was the look of desperation. She was in pain. Her worries were not irrational. Her concerns were valid. I understood too well the aching inside her heart that can only be described as longing. She sighed and asked her question again, "What am I supposed to do next?" Her words fell on ears that have heard the same sentiment many times before—the only difference was the name of the person who sat in front of me. And her face.

There had been many others. They had each come to me after a particular breaking point—one I was familiar with. It was typically after watching another friend experience a breakthrough or, at the very least, an answer to prayer. While they were excited for their friends' promotions, relationships, and open doors, they also felt confused, hurt, and afraid. Why were others feeling a sense of direction from the Lord—and they were not? It wasn't for lack of praying and listening earnestly. They were desperate to receive the answers to their questions, their pleas, their dilemmas, but the only response was quiet. The stillness was not what they were seeking. They were hungry for the next step yet unable to see past the fork in the road. They were eager to get going but unsure of which direction to take. They were afraid of messing up God's plan for their lives, of walking outside of His will, of missing something if they didn't move quickly enough. It's not a new dilemma, but one that humans have wrestled with since the garden.

"Now what, God?" is a question I have asked often. In the quiet, I hear my own voice, the one that spoke softly to Danielle all those years ago, say, *"What was the last thing you remember Him asking you to do?"* and the gentle follow-up, *"Did you do it?"*

This is the advice I have dispensed often, believing that God doesn't change His mind, nor is He the One who moves away from us. If God seems silent and the path before us seems unclear, there could be several reasons why, but none of them cast the blame at God.

– – –

About a year and a half after I quit my day job, our family packed up to relocate from one end of the state to the other. My husband had taken a new position, which meant a major life change for our family. Because we were already in a place where we weren't dependent on a second income, where home education was the norm, and where Mommy was home to steady the ship as it rocked back and forth in a transitional season, the jump into new life was less "bumpy" and more exciting. We moved in the middle of the spring and instantly dove into growing community and establishing ourselves in a new city.

Within months, however, I was struggling with the idea of going back to work part-time, citing that I wanted to be the "most productive" with my time and skills. It was my husband who graciously (but forcefully) reminded me, over and over, that I had felt God ask me to write the words you're reading right now, and until I completed that assignment, He wasn't going to bless anything else I put my hand to. My sweet husband was all of a sudden giving me the "obedience over hustle" sermon, and I'm so glad he did. He is the one who gave me permission and freedom to pen these words, acknowledging, "If you get a part-time job, you're never going to finish writing this thing." It was what my heart needed—not just the validation that I *could* do it, but that I *should*; I needed to obey what I felt God had already asked me to do.

Most of the time we don't want to admit when we haven't finished what God has asked us to do. We can try to move forward, but typically we find ourselves running in circles, avoiding whatever it is that He last spoke to us. I had no business dreaming and scheming about what I *could be* doing when I hadn't completed the last thing God had asked me to do.

— — —

Not everyone can have a moment of burning bush clarity like Moses did or an angelic visitation or dream like Joseph did. We aren't all living the story of Daniel, faced with obeying God or bowing to a human leader. Not everyone has a situation like Noah or Paul, where God hands down an odd or enormous task for us to tackle with precision or expediency.

Often what we are faced with choosing is option number one or option number two. One path may seem more appealing for a certain reason, but that is not always the case. And when we are left with a decision to make and God seems silent on the matter, then I believe He is leaving us to use our best judgment.

This is where we find Luke the physician[98]—the man who penned the words of the Gospel named after himself. Unlike other books for which God instructed a prophet, king, or apostle to pick up a pen as He began to dictate stories and visions of the future, Luke did not have such an encounter. In fact, the Gospel of Luke came to be because this doctor set out to write down what he had observed from eyewitness accounts and testimonies:

> *Many people have set out to write accounts about the events that have been fulfilled among us. They used the eyewitness reports circulating among us from the early disciples. Having carefully investigated everything from the beginning, I also have decided to write an accurate account for you, most honorable Theophilus, so you can be certain of the truth of everything you were taught.*[99]

Simply stated, it reads like this: *"I had this idea, and it sounded like a good one. So I researched it and put pen to paper."*

Luke was doing what God had wired him to do. He was a learned man with an affinity for deep thinking and investigation. It wasn't a grandiose act for a physician to keep records or dive into research about an ailment and its remedy. Luke decided to apply that same thirst for

---

[98] Colossians 4:14

[99] Luke 1:1–4 NLT

knowledge and information to the story of Jesus. Doing so helped to preserve the account of Jesus' life and ministry so that others would be able to read about it for the rest of time. Luke was using the same gifts and abilities that probably drove him to be a doctor to do something different, even though we have no reason to believe that God showed up and asked him to write a book of the Bible.

Was this a good idea for Luke? Absolutely! Are there other things he *could have* been doing with his time and abilities? Probably so. He used his best judgment and the result is a book of the Bible that people around the world turn to every Christmas. He probably didn't start out wondering if his writing project would bring him fame. His intention was to write down the story, to make it available to others—to share the good news of Jesus.

— — —

Sometimes we get unusually worked up about what it means to be "in the will of God," fearful that one decision will somehow cause a wrinkle in the fabric of our lives or, even worse, affect others in a terrible way. My husband always likes to lighten the mood during such emotionally charged conversations and remind people, "It's a lot harder to fall out of the will of God than you think." Often he is met with a look of shock and awe at the thought, and his response is, "If you're pursuing a relationship with Jesus, then how can you fall out of His will? That would be like me pursuing a life of romance with my wife and suddenly waking up fearing that we're going to fall out of love. It doesn't work that way." (I just love that man!)

There is an incorrect assumption in some Christian

circles that God is intentionally withholding information from us, that to know His will for our lives means to have to sequester ourselves for long periods of prayer and fasting to discern what He wants us to do next. God isn't a dictator holding all the cards and waiting for us to make a misstep. He isn't a Father who will punish us if we get a little off course or need to u-turn at some point because what we *thought* was a good decision didn't turn out to be that great after all.

For a brief season my husband and I were student pastors. We thought we were moving in God's will when we assumed the roles we did, but within a short time it was clear we wouldn't be able to stay long as we were having to teach things we didn't agree with and condone behavior that we knew was not pleasing to God. While others may see this time in our lives as a mistake—wrongfully stepping into these positions—we view it as an incredible learning experience. The most beautiful part is that many of the students we led are now in full-time ministry, some are married with children, and most of them are in healthy churches. We tended to the people God gave us influence over the best way we knew how, and we matured a lot in that season. We were reminded of strengths and gifts inside of us that had been dormant for a while, and we were able to stretch and grow as leaders responsible for students of all ages as well as adult volunteers. Because we were pursuing God, it was easy to make the decision to leave when we could no longer, in good conscience, stay.

Sometimes we make a decision only to realize that though it isn't horrible, it is far from "healthy." It may be a relationship, a job situation, or a location that we were once excited about, but the longer we stay, the more we recognize that it isn't the best option for us and something needs to change. It doesn't mean we've messed up or that there will be a consequence due to our poor decision. Remember, God doesn't waste anything. He isn't angry with us when we need to pull back, reassess a situation, or make a switch that could be tumultuous for ourselves and others. When we are following Him, when we are in relationship with Him, these blips in our story are less like crashes and more like "the long way around."

Other times the path before us may appear to be long and without much scenery. What we are looking for is the route full of excitement and adventure, and what God wants us to tackle is "doing well in school," "being an attentive mom," or "being a trustworthy employee." It doesn't mean there are no *great big things* for us to do (like our parents and youth pastors have been telling us since we were children); it means that *for now* His plan is to grow us and mature us through the beautifully mundane parts of life that almost everyone lives through. Whether we survive or thrive in those seasons is solely up to us.

- - -

The more time you spend with God, the better you will know what He wants you to do. Sometimes His words will simply be to "continue on," and other times He may point you in a direction that looks terrifying and out of left field. And then there will be moments when He asks you to "go back and finish what you started." God is always interested in the journey, not just the destination; He wants us to complete the last thing well, having learned the lesson and gleaned all the wisdom we could so that we are ready for the next assignment.

CHAPTER 17

Obedience: Not Just Direction but Pace

*T*he right thing, at the wrong time, is the wrong thing.*" I'm
not sure who coined that phrase, but I can recall where I
was sitting when I heard it. I was a college-aged student in
a room full of hundreds of my peers, listening to a talk on
romantic relationships. The speaker was using the quote as
a way to drive home their point: "Just because God has told
you who you're going to spend the rest of your life with
doesn't mean you've got the green light to go out and get
married tomorrow." I remember jotting the words in my
journal, because at that particular moment I was sure that
my future husband was sitting in the same room, just a few
rows away. Ours was really an impossible situation, as I was
in his country on a student visa and would be returning
to Canada within months, but I was fairly sure that God
would bring us together again one day, even though I knew
God wasn't blessing a romantic relationship at that time.

For me, the phrase wasn't just a casual statement that
you write on a sticky note and leave on your mirror; those
words were carved into my heart. They've been something I've lived my life by ever since. (As for the guy in
the room—yes, we were married a couple of years after
hearing that relationship talk.) I've recited the words over
and over and quoted them to those I've walked with and
mentored—to new believers and mature Christians. *The
right thing, at the wrong time, is the wrong thing.*

In that same season of my life, I had a mentor who once told me to hold loosely my ideas of my future. I had just come back from a vision retreat where we had been asked to create a mission statement for our lives. As a writer, I found the "one sentence" assignment to be challenging, but the weekend itself was beautiful. Not only were we fasting from food for the entirety of the retreat, but we had also taken a vow of silence. The only time we were verbal was during our corporate worship sessions sprinkled throughout the weekend. The rest of the time we spent in quiet reflection, prayer, and journaling sessions. Some people napped (I think my husband was probably part of that group), but for an introvert and writer, it was a gift and a dream scenario.

Fresh from the retreat, I was filled with grandiose ideas and carved-in-stone plans for what I felt God had downloaded to me; I was so passionate. I still have those words, perfectly typed up and preserved. For fun, I recently dug them out and studied them. The writing itself was a tad embarrassing, but reading the words was rewarding as I recognized that many of those God-dreams had already come to pass, even if they looked different in real life than the phrases I had used to describe them in my college days.

That's what my mentor intended—not to squelch my passion, but to teach me that God's plans are God's. They are not mine to mold and manipulate. God's timing is perfect, and often my unmet expectations (and resulting emotional frustrations) through the years have occurred when I tried to hurry His hand.

Her encouragement was that, while God had given me

a word for my future, I should be prepared for it to unfold differently from the way my finite mind expected—I should not try to fit it into my five-year plan. "Just because God created you to be a teacher, for example, doesn't mean it will be with teaching credentials or in front of a classroom of pupils. It may look very different, and perhaps He means later in your years when you can teach from life experience, or maybe it will be a life of teaching completed as a parent, mentor, or boss." While *teacher* was not a word that I had heard that week, I understood what she was saying, even if my ego was a little hurt by the reality of her words.

We tend to think that the deposited dream is permission to hustle toward the goal. And to a degree, God does expect us to move if He's given us a goal—we've already discussed this. God wants us to possess a good work ethic, to be those whom He can entrust with stupendous plans. He wants us to be able to dig deep, work hard, and produce results, but He doesn't want us becoming slaves to our work or sacrificing relationships in the process.

The *how* of God's plans is for Him to dictate, just like the *when*. If He has called you to be a speaker, a teacher, or a mother, it won't necessarily happen tomorrow, or next year, or within the next decade. Obedience to God means that we surrender not only to His plan but also to His timeline.

— — —

Of all the characters we see throughout Scripture, a couple of men stand out as those who knew how to embrace not only God's plan but also His pace. Joseph is the first.

No doubt many of us who read the account of Joseph

in Genesis feel understood when we hear that at age seventeen[100] he had a dream about his future.[101] We enjoy knowing that God brought the dream to fruition and set Joseph up as a powerful leader, yet we sometimes skim over the fact that it took many years for the plan to unfold. And rather than falling into the pit of self-pity and accusing God for not following through and bringing the dream to fruition, Joseph rolled up his sleeves and got busy—first as a slave.

He had been sold by his own brothers,[102] sent away to be forgotten forever, only to find favor in the eyes of his master Potiphar.[103] He rose to become the head of his master's home, successful in all he put his hand to. Unfortunately, the story continues with the sexual assault accusation[104] that lands him in prison.[105]

Again, Joseph chose not to curl up in the fetal position, overanalyze his situation, or rage against Potiphar for believing his wife's lies, or against God for allowing this to happen to him. Even in Joseph's negative circumstances, God had favor on him and he quickly rose to a place of leadership underneath the warden.[106] The favor he received seemed to do little for his situation, however; he was forgotten[107] and remained locked up for many years. The Bible says Joseph was thirty years old when he was plucked out

---

[100] Genesis 37:2

[101] Genesis 37:5

[102] Genesis 37:28

[103] Genesis 37:36

[104] Genesis 39:17–18

[105] Genesis 39:20

[106] Genesis 39:21–23

[107] Genesis 40:23

of prison and established as the second in command underneath Pharaoh.[108]

Perhaps Joseph's story is difficult for you to read because you know the sting of hope deferred. Maybe you've been waiting for years, or as with Joseph, maybe you've been waiting for decades. My question to you is, What have you been doing in the meantime?

The life story of another biblical character reminds me of what it looks like to trust God's pace. It's the story of King David—before he took the throne.

If ever there was someone in the Bible who could have hustled to "get what had been promised," it's David. He had been anointed as a young man[109] to become the king of God's people, a strange thing since King Saul was currently sitting on the throne. It would be many years, however, before young David assumed the throne—not until he was a thirty year old man.[110]

David was content to let God write his story. Instead of becoming bitter that his time hadn't yet come, he continued to do whatever was before him to do: tend the flocks of his father,[111] write songs and lead people in worship,[112] and be the armor bearer to the current king.[113] There is nothing overtly special about any of these roles. None of them was really a stepping-stone to becoming king. The progression from tending sheep to leading a nation isn't really a natural

---

[108] Genesis 41:41–46

[109] 1 Samuel 16:11

[110] 2 Samuel 5:4

[111] 1 Samuel 17:34

[112] 1 Samuel 16:23

[113] 1 Samuel 16:21

one, but that is exactly what happened.

God didn't waste a single moment in either Joseph's or David's life. Everything they endured, every lesson, each opportunity, was part of a greater plan. At times we need to remember that God's plan for our life *is* the greater plan—it's not the end He cares about so much as what's happening inside of us along the way. He is just as eager to see us tend to our families (as David tended to sheep) as He is to see us lead thousands. He's watching as intently when we serve in obscurity as when we are standing in front of a massive audience. God is just as concerned about the words we speak to ourselves as the words we put out there for the internet to consume. That's why there is often a pause between what is whispered to our hearts and what comes to fruition.

Often we become hyper-focused on the dream or the plan. Sometimes that happens when well-meaning parents, teachers, coaches, or other leaders practically shove us into a calling based on the natural gifts they see in our lives. Others of us have an actual dream or vision from the Lord about the way our future is going to look. But just because the future seems to be clear doesn't mean that it is immediate. Joseph and David each waited a period of thirteen to twenty years before God felt that their character, heart, and skills were up to the job ahead.

Just because God has given you a plan (even with precise details) doesn't mean He has given you the green light to make it happen now. When we attempt to do that, we tend to make a mess. Look at the Abraham, Sarah, Hagar triangle and all the turmoil it caused—that we can read about. Undoubtedly much more drama occurred in those relationships, as well as within the rest of their camp, not to mention the strife created between the two step-brothers and the generations to come. When we take it upon ourselves to make God's plans happen on our time-line, we produce Ishmaels instead of Isaacs; a lot of people get hurt as a result, and the fallout can be devastating and far-reaching.

Instead of forcing God's hand, we need to exercise patience. Rather than whine that what God promised us hasn't come to fruition, we need to be mindful of our lim-ited vantage point. What He sees is far beyond what we can understand. We not only need to obey when He tells us to move, but need to stay when He says, "Be still." In all things, we need to trust that His timing is perfect. God has never made a mistake, so if He hasn't moved you into the promised land yet, perhaps you haven't finished learning what it is He sent you into the wilderness to learn.

Let me offer one final thought: maybe your delay isn't about what God is protecting you from, but rather He has something else He needs you to do first. Just because He's saying "wait" doesn't mean you have nothing to do. Perhaps He wants you to focus on your children or to love your spouse in a way that makes the neighbors ask after your secret to a happy marriage. Maybe God's plan is for you to serve in obscurity at your church for a season—not to make an impression on leadership or to advance, but because He wants you to learn how to serve well. Maybe He wants to see you roll up your sleeves and work on that temper (yes, you—with the book-throwing issue), or forgive your parents, or become an avid student of the Bible or the prayer warrior you've always wanted to be.

What would have happened if God had taken the cocky seventeen-year-old Joseph and given him the "second in command" title? Do you think David was ready to assume the role of king as an adolescent? There was a purpose to what God allowed to happen. There were other things He had for both men—lessons, tests, character development that had to be wrestled with and worked out. David learned how to worship God despite his circumstances; he learned to trust God and overcome fear (hello, fight against a lion!). Joseph had to learn what it meant to have no one believe him (false accusations can be devastating) and to develop a solid work ethic regardless of where that work was located.

For some of you reading, this is the most uncomfortable chapter because you know that God has been speaking specific things to your heart for a long time—and you've been ignoring Him. Maybe He has told you to "wait"—on building that business, writing the book, moving overseas, starting your family—and you've been pushing forward with a fire in your heart. Perhaps it's something else you've felt you need to do—like finding a counselor and working through some past hurts or trauma, or reconciling with a family member or old friend—yet you've been avoiding doing so and making excuses. For some, the gentle nudging of the Lord has been to serve at church, on your street, in your home, and that just doesn't feel like *enough*. It's not picture worthy, and it won't give you any line items on your résumé worth mentioning, but—*you know what I'm going to respond with*—does any of that matter?

Delay doesn't mean denial, friend. And just because God has whispered, "Wait," doesn't mean you have nothing to do. It's time for us to stop feeling sorry for ourselves

because of the dream that has not yet materialized and remember that God's dream for our lives is *right now*. Today
is what we are held accountable for—the people entrusted
to us, the positions we currently hold, the daily possibilities
that present themselves. What are you doing with what
you have right now?

CHAPTER 18

Exchanging Fear for Obedience

Gideon chokes as hundreds and then thousands of men turn and walk away. At first they shyly slipped away in groups, but now it has turned into a mass exodus. He motions to an attendant and asks for a new head count of the men who have remained.

The lingering troops are sent off for food and rest, and when the number is finally reported to Gideon, the blood drains from his face. The ground beneath him seems to sway, and quickly he reaches for his armor bearer to steady him. With swift movements the man embraces his leader, ushering him into a tent and ordering cool water to be brought at once. Through a small opening, Gideon watches as tens of thousands of soldiers retreat into the distance, each one headed home.

"Lord, it should be me walking with those men!" he cries out inwardly. "I'm the one who is trembling in fear. Why can't I go home too?" he questions.

Just then a young boy enters the tent with cold water. His armor bearer takes it and sends the boy out, embarrassed for his master to be seen in such a vulnerable position.

"Here, drink this. It will refresh you," the man says as he stoops over Gideon's body, battling his own questions about whether this man has what it will take to lead the remaining men against the enemy armies.

He watches as Gideon drinks deeply and then

lies back, eyes turned heavenward as if searching the ceiling for the face of God. The armor bearer excuses himself from the tent, leaving Gideon alone and still wrestling with his fears.

— — —

*D*o you have a favorite Bible character? I do. Honestly, I have several. There are many individuals whose life lessons, personality quirks, and stories I can identify with. I love Peter, with his lack of a filter and quick-to-react temperament; Paul, with his obsession for the church to be healthy and well equipped; and Abraham, who learned patience in the midst of moving to a foreign land. While there are many great kings and prophets to learn from and be inspired by, it is the story of Gideon's life in the book of Judges that I have returned to over and over. I understand his fears and insecurities. I've wept over the pages of my Bible while reading the familiar lines that have Gideon begging God repeatedly for confirmation.

Unlike many others, Gideon's list of accomplishments and personal traits is relatively short; his entire life is told in just a few chapters. The beginning of the book of Judges chronicles the steps that God took to get Gideon in the game—the painstaking journey that started with a small, doubtful, fearful man hiding in a winepress[114] and ended with him becoming one of the great heroes of the Old Testament.

As I read the chapters that tell his story, I realize that God saw something in Gideon that he was unable to see

---

[114] Judges 6:11–12

on his own. Not only that, but God was eager and yet so patient with Gideon as he took the baby steps from coward to warrior. God did not push Gideon aside when he got mouthy and started questioning the infinite wisdom and plan of God. He spoke to Gideon directly and often with great detail about the plans He had drawn up. Yet even with all the confirmations and miracles God provided, Gideon still asked for more. In one story, Gideon responds to God with these words: "*Me*, my master? How and with what could I ever save Israel? Look at me. My clan's the weakest in Manasseh and I'm the runt of the litter."[115]

Maybe that sounds familiar: *I have no skills. I am not smart enough. I never finished college. I grew up on the wrong side of the tracks. I don't have any experience. I have a past full of mistakes. My family doesn't have any money. I am divorced. My heritage is not noteworthy.*

You are not alone. Most of the phrases above could have been copied line by line from one of my journals. Typically, one of these outbursts comes on the heels of a magnificent mountaintop experience where I heard God's voice clearly or saw His hand moving in or through my life. One side of the page abounds with testimony of God's goodness and provision, and the other teems with question marks, doubt, and discouragement.

What I love about Gideon's story is that you never read about God changing His mind. He doesn't find someone else, kicking Gideon to the curb. He doesn't miraculously provide Gideon with a new brain that can fully compre-hend the plans of God. Gideon's lack of faith seems to be

---

[115] Judges 6:15 MSG

a nonissue, a fact that is of great comfort to me. Regardless of how Gideon pictured himself, God saw him through a different lens, and that's why He showered him with the words "Brave warrior." He let Gideon linger in his doubts and fears, and when he presented a series of hoops for God to jump through, God obliged him. But once the tests had been passed, God expected movement from Gideon in return.

After God had produced fire from nothing,[116] kept the ground wet and the fleece dry, and then the ground dry and the fleece wet,[117] it was time for Gideon to put on his big-boy pants and get to the task at hand. Gideon started with only ten men, but he was soon surrounded by more than thirty-two thousand soldiers! By some miracle, he had managed to gather an army, but before they launched into full battle mode, God interrupted the planning to make a few changes to the ranks. He said: *"You have too many warriors with you. . . . Tell the people, 'Whoever is timid or afraid may leave this mountain and go home.'"*[118]

Twenty-two thousand men stepped forward timidly when Gideon asked who among them was afraid. They had no idea they were about to be sent back to their families. When Gideon gave the orders for these scaredy-cats to pack their belongings and return home, there must have been smiles and fist bumps all around. They shrugged their shoulders at their friends who were too proud to admit their fear and doubt, and they kicked up their feet as they began the journey home. Some of them wiped sweat from

---

[116] Judges 6:21

[117] Judges 6:36–40 NLT

[118] Judges 7:2–3 NLT

their brows as they struggled to concoct an honorable story to tell their families about their early release.

Those who remained stood taller, with slightly larger egos and chests puffed out a bit farther. While those who remained appeared to be the confident and chosen ones, God knew something else. Maybe he was looking for the pure-hearted, those without pride in their eyes. Perhaps He wanted to be rid of those bloodthirsty few instead of having them lead the charge. Whatever His reasons, God looked over the ranks and made yet another cut. The second group of ten thousand fighters was told to pack their bags and return home; and there Gideon stood with his God-approved army of only three hundred men.

You would think that at this point God had spoken so plainly and with so much detail that Gideon would be sure of his ability to hear and know the voice of the Lord. But he wasn't.

Maybe it was seeing tens of thousands of men walk away that caused Gideon to panic. Perhaps he found himself envious of those who were free to return home, unscathed from the inevitable battle. His hands started sweating and his heartbeat accelerated, and into his mind wandered thoughts that had been silent only moments ago: *Who do you think you are? You are the least, the smallest, the weakest. Who are you to lead this tiny band of men against such a powerful army?* Or maybe they came on stronger: *Hey, Gideon, what are you going to do now? You've lost your army. Are you sure God said to send that group home? Maybe you got it wrong. I'm sure God meant to send home the three hundred and keep the group of ten thousand—what were you thinking?!*

Apply this situation to a modern-day scenario and it

looks like deleting all but one-tenth of your email list on the eve of a giant product launch, a grand opening, a book release, or the biggest speech of your life. It would be like God walking into your living room and saying, "Get rid of 90 percent of your social media followers." Maybe you're a church planter, you've started a ministry, you're in the midst of an international adoption, or you're gearing up for a major career change. How would it feel if God took away all but a handful of your support system in one day?

Would you do it? Would you obey in the face of such great risk, or would you drown out God's voice and go about your business as usual? Would you let God do things His way, or would you respond with a list of reasons why it won't work and you aren't the best candidate?

Maybe you've stood in a similar place as Gideon. God asked you to take a leap of faith and you started out eagerly, but before long, fear pummeled you. Doubt attacked, and you were left in the fetal position, wondering why you'd said yes in the first place. This is where Gideon stood.

I envision Gideon doing the same song and dance that he did a chapter earlier, "God, You've got the wrong guy. The last thing You had me do was a breeze in comparison to what You're asking me to do now. There's no way I'm equipped for this task. And You just sent away 90 percent of my help. God, I hate to correct You again, but I think You picked the wrong man. This isn't how I'm wired; I don't even like fighting!"

Regardless of the dialogue, God saw Gideon's fear. It was all over his face, thumping inside his chest, the melody on repeat in his mind—doubt, doubt, doubt, worry, fear, anxiety, questions, more doubt. So what did God do? Guilt Gideon for doubting? Shame him for second-guessing?

Kick him while he was down?

No. He came near. He got close. Close enough for Gideon to hear His whisper, to sense His power, to know the weight of His presence. He pressed Himself into the space around Gideon and spoke the truth to his heart. And then God sent Gideon into the enemy camp to receive confirmation of the plan He had laid out.

Did you catch that?

I don't want you to miss that small detail, the one thought I missed so many times in reading these passages: God sent Gideon into the enemy's camp. Why? To gain the necessary courage to defeat his foes. God not only allowed it to happen but paved the way for Gideon to get what he needed: confirmation and courage.

Maybe you're guilty, as I have been, not necessarily of walking into the enemy's camp looking for confirmation, but of running to friends, mentors, and leaders for advice. Many of us have had moments when we doubted our ability to make the right decision or were unsure of whether we were capable of doing what God had asked us to do. During times like these, in our fear, we run to others. Like Gideon, we tend to be eager to hear the whispers of man when we have already heard the voice of God. But still, God is patient with us, just as He was with our Bible hero.

With his armor bearer at his side, Gideon stealthily crept down into the enemy camp under the cover of darkness. As they were crouching behind a tent, they heard the muffled voices of men in the very army they planned to attack:

A man was telling his companion about a dream. The

*man said, "I had this dream, and in my dream a loaf
of barley bread came tumbling down into the Midi-
anite camp. It hit a tent, turned it over, and knocked
it flat!"*

*His companion answered, "Your dream can mean
only one thing—God has given Gideon son of Joash,
the Israelite, victory over Midian and all its allies!"*[119]

I can visualize Gideon's armor bearer giving him a punch
and a wink as they slipped through the shadows back the
way they had come. With adrenaline and courage suddenly
pumping through their veins, they eagerly rejoined their
troops to fight this battle that God had positioned them to
win. Gideon gathered the men around and gave them their
orders, unconventional as they were. They went to battle with their torches and horns, and Gideon won. God's
people were victorious, and a fear of the "Israelite God"
fell over the land once again.

Three chapters in Judges: a couple of victories and a
huge triumph for God's people. But the story isn't about
the defeat of Midian as much as it is about God's win over
Gideon's heart. And the way one fearful little man stepped
up into his God-given role, even though he was teeming
with questions and doubts and shaking in his boots the
entire time.

Here is the question: If God calls you "brave warrior," regardless of your circumstances, who are you to say
otherwise? Why aren't those words enough? Why are we
so fearful of stepping out in obedience to do what He's

---

[119] Judges 7:13–14 NLT

asked us to do? Why do we need to hear it from the lips of mortal men before we choose to believe what our all-knowing Father has spoken to us?

Many of us have no problem trusting God when it's just Him and us. He gives us a dream, a plan, a vision, and we scribble it down, share it with a friend or a spouse, and spend time researching the causes He has dropped in our hearts. But when we have to actually step out in faith and start the ministry, quit the job, or change the way we handle and give our money, we tend to step back instead. It's in those moments we go searching for confirmation—we ask for prayer, for wisdom, instead of walking courageously into what God has asked us to do.

Has God spoken plainly to you recently and your response was to turn away and ask another human for their thoughts and wisdom? Have you been guilty of stalking the whispers of the Enemy instead of heading boldly in the direction God has asked you to go? Are you ready to move forward, even in the unconventional plans God has given you, with courage? It's time for us to move from fear to obedience.

CHAPTER 19

Courageous Obedience

And he said to the people, "Go forward. March around the city and let the armed men pass on before the ark of the LORD."

—JOSHUA 6:7 ESV

"Don't get too excited, guys; I've heard that Joshua doesn't intend for us to fight."

"Doesn't want us to fight?! Then why did he call up the armed men? What are we preparing for?"

"I heard his plan is for us to march around Jericho."

"March around the walls? You can't be serious!"

"I am. We are to go before and behind the ark while the priests blow their horns."

"Do we at least get to sound the battle cry?"

" 'Fraid not. Joshua plans to have us march around the city in silence."

"I hope Joshua has a backup plan, because this idea sounds ridiculous."

Ridiculous idea. Ever heard one of those? I have.

They come in moments when you are sure that God is, indeed, giving you specific directions. His voice is clearer than it has ever been, yet you are left shaking because the thing He has asked you to do sounds, well. . . ridiculous. These ideas might sound like God telling you to quit your job, shut down your business, or start something you're totally unqualified to do but incredibly passionate about. They may sound like bizarre and outlandish plans, but that tends to be where God resides—in the land of the wild and miraculous. And that was the exact place a young Israelite leader found himself in chapter 6 of the book of Joshua.

For most of us, when we hear the name "Joshua," our first thought is "Jericho." We've heard the story since we were young, perhaps read to us from a children's Bible or even acted out by Larry the Cucumber. We know how Joshua gathered the people and gave them specific directions for marching silently and then returning to camp, not once or twice, but six times. And how on the seventh day they circled the city of Jericho seven times and finally, under a great cacophony of shouting people, the walls of the enemy city crumbled at their feet.[120]

It is a story of God rescuing His people in such a way that He received credit for the victory as the people stood back, amazed at His power. And while the story of Jericho is one of significance in Joshua's life, there was an earlier moment when he was required to walk courageously into the plan God had for him, as ridiculous as it sounded. And perhaps it's the reason why marching silently around the walls of an enemy city were orders that Joshua didn't seem to blink at.

Before the Israelites came to the city of Jericho, they had to cross over the Jordan River. This wasn't the first time God had sent His people to a shore with a plan to part the

---

waters for them. Moses was the first one to have a front-row seat when God made a dry path in the middle of a seabed. Moses was able to stand back and witness the power of God, but Joshua's situation was different. Before moving his people through the Jordan River, Joshua was given the following instructions:

> "And when the soles of the feet of the priests bearing the ark of the LORD, the Lord of all the earth, shall rest in the waters of the Jordan, the waters of the Jordan shall be cut off from flowing, and the waters coming down from above shall stand in one heap."[121]

Joshua's orders came directly from God. And so he had a choice. We will probably never know if any words were exchanged or if Joshua had any doubts. We aren't told whether He challenged God's ideas or consulted his wife to see if she had peace about what God had spoken to him. If it had been me, I would have done a couple of laps in the anxiety pool, called my husband to have him talk me off the cliff, and then gathered some friends to pray with me. Anyone else?

There may have even been a moment when Joshua wished for the miracle to be performed the way God did it for Moses: with a staff held over the water and dry ground that materialized before they had to actively engage in the miracle. Because when faced with the need for a miracle, we tend to want to tell God how to do it. We love being witness to the miracle, but we don't always love the vantage

---

[121] Joshua 3:13 ESV

point He wants us to experience it from.

It certainly didn't make sense—to step out into a flowing river, a river that was "going over its banks."[122] But that's exactly what Joshua sent the priests to do. And "as soon as they stepped out on dry ground, the water of the Jordan began to flow again. It went over its banks, just as it had done before."[123]

Joshua's mentor, Moses, had to have tremendous faith—to believe that God *could* part the waters and *would* follow through, keeping two million people safe as they crossed to the other side. But stepping out into a flooded river seems to necessitate even greater faith than that of Moses.

So how did Joshua get it? Was he more gifted in the area of faith than Moses (the man whose face glowed brightly after being in God's presence)?[124] Surely not. Did he wake up one morning with a more generous helping of belief? Or is the more likely reason for his tremendous faith that he had been given the experience of watching God's miracles as Moses' apprentice? With his own eyes, Joshua had seen God show up, provide, and prove His strength, over and over. All the wondrous signs in Egypt and then another forty years of daily provision and continued miracles reinforced Joshua's confidence. Of the twelve spies sent into the Promised Land, he was one of only two to see its eventual possession by the Israelites.[125] It's clear that God was doing a work in Joshua's heart during those years

[122] Joshua 3:15 NIRV

[123] Joshua 4:18 NIRV

[124] Exodus 34:29

[125] Numbers 14:30

in the wilderness—allowing His voice to become crystal clear and Joshua to become resolute when it came to obeying God's commands. Because that's how God works—stretching our faith a little bit at a time, His voice becoming clearer and clearer until one day God is asking us to step bravely into a flooded river.

In Joshua 1 we hear God say, "Do not be afraid," repeatedly. He encouraged Joshua to be full of courage. Joshua was unable to predict what the future would hold; he couldn't fathom the enemies God intended for him to battle, the victories he would inevitably experience, but God knew. He saw what was ahead for Joshua and decided to equip him, speaking the necessary courage into his heart. For God knew that what would be required of this servant would be even greater than Moses' faith.

While Moses saw the parting of the Red Sea, it was a gradual (over the course of hours) miracle as the wind of God blew back the waters into walls that curtained the Israelite exit.[126] For Joshua, however, the Jordan River ran wildly. The flow didn't diminish to a trickle; the winds didn't blow in from the east as they did for Moses.[127] In fact, the waters stopped flowing at another point in the river, at another place "a great distance away"[128] from the point at which they crossed; they didn't get to "see" the walls of water like those who had crossed the Red Sea did. Moses could see a path that was dry and unobstructed; Joshua could see only teeming waters. No path, no walkway, no direction but *through* it. The directions he gave to the priests

---

[126] Exodus 14:21–22

[127] Exodus 14:21

[128] Joshua 3:16 NIV

were, "Go and *stand in* the river."[129] Talk about needing an extra dose of courage that day!

Have you ever felt like that? Has God ever asked you to go stand in a place that caused you to question whether you had the courage necessary to do it? That's how I felt when God asked me to obey—to walk away from my job and trust Him to provide for us. It seemed ridiculous. And as the days and weeks passed, I felt like I was standing in the midst of a rushing river that was *not* drying up. But I continued to stand in my decision and in the knowledge that God promised to take care of us. I stretched my faith muscles, telling myself that He wouldn't lead me to this decision (to the river) and then not provide (let me drown).

Joshua may have been able to find another route, and there are other miracles God *could have* performed. I think it's interesting that He chose something the Israelites were already familiar with—but He upped the ante. He expected their faith to be stronger because they had already borne witness to such an incredible miracle. Stepping into the river built Joshua's faith and the faith of every person he was charged with leading.

It was not enough that Joshua had been a part of great miracles in the past. God was doing something new. That's part of His nature. But He's always building on what has happened in the past. His plan is to take us to greater places of faith, which will require a more courageous obedience.

It takes courageous obedience to step into a flooded river with faith that the waters will recede.

---

[129] Joshua 3:8 NIV (emphasis mine)

It takes courageous obedience to quit the dream job to stay home full-time as a mother.

It takes courageous obedience to work toward your God-dream when it opposes the American dream.

It takes courageous obedience to believe for the adoption when all the whispers say it's expensive and time-consuming.

It takes courageous obedience to quit school and put all your effort into getting your business up and running.

It takes courageous obedience to say yes to what God has asked us to do sometimes.

But if we don't, then will He ever ask us to do anything else?

Sometimes our most memorable moments of faith—those daunting situations where we feel like we are about to risk everything and free-fall—are as much about increasing the faith of those we are leading as increasing our own. When others see *you* walking in faith, they are encouraged too. The journey probably looks different, as do the specific directions God gives each to obey, but what others catch as they watch you step out into your river is the message, "If she can do it, then so can I." Your courage empowers others to move in the direction God is leading them. Remember, God didn't just tell Joshua to get going on a solo mission. The direction was for him "and all this people" to cross the Jordan.[130] Rarely does God have us move forward so we can go on a solo adventure; often we are supposed to take others with us.

So what has God asked you to do? Maybe it isn't to

---

[130] Joshua 1:2 ESV

step out into a flooded river, but His task could be just as petrifying for you. The choice may not seem to have such potentially dire consequences, and chances are you don't have hundreds of thousands of followers watching your next move (or maybe you do?). But the stakes are just as high because obedience isn't as much about the physical step as it is the heart that surrenders to God's voice. What we've seen God do in our lives to this point has served to get us ready for what's coming next. As we face what lies before us, may we choose courageous obedience—even in the midst of fear.

CHAPTER 20

Fruitful Obedience

*Q*uitting my day job was one of the riskiest things I've ever done. It was a career that I had worked through school to pay for, one that provided me with self-fulfillment, and one that, most days, I genuinely enjoyed. From a financial standpoint, the jump we took appeared quite foolish (and some people were so kind to point that out to us). Our family had just moved into a rental home (a sizable difference from our two-bedroom apartment), which came with a 30 percent increase in our monthly expenses. At that time, we lived in a very affluent area, and my hardworking husband worked for a church (not exactly an executive salary). When I quit my job, we expected a decrease of 30 percent in our monthly income. The math didn't make sense, but we did it anyway.

My husband called it God math. Most people would call it crazy because I quit one month before Christmas—the most expensive season of the year. We gathered our close friends and family to stand with us in prayer, believing that God would meet our needs, and we moved forward in courageous faith. It was unnerving, but we were confident that God was asking us to flex our faith muscles and that He alone would meet our needs. And somehow, in the middle of our crazy reality, we went to sleep at night in peace.

In the first month of the new year, there was no change

to our financial situation. It was discouraging, as I had expected that God would open a door and hand me a work-from-home job to help balance the budget. After all, I had obeyed and quit my job. We had taken a huge leap of faith and had anticipated that God would "provide" for us in a specific way—with me working from home, of course. There were days filled with anxiety over where the money would come from, but rather than becoming consumed with fear, I continued to surrender. I told God He could do it however He wanted, and I poured myself into those *few* things that He had told me to do.

Homeschooling our children was the first thing on my list, and the others were building a community and embracing the discipline of writing. I enrolled in classes to sharpen my skills and grew bold in submitting my words to a variety of publications—even if no payment was involved. While I really wanted to influence others, God reminded me that a bigger audience means nothing to Him. He asked me to love my neighbors well, to open our doors regularly, and to eventually mentor a small group of college students. Interestingly, my words started getting published, both online and in print. Requests started rolling in to contribute to devotionals, magazines, and blogs. Then came requests to share at a MOPs event, teach an online class, and speak at a women's retreat. Slowly, over time, I started to see momentum, even though I didn't see paychecks.

However, something else interesting did happen. My husband (who is a lighting and scenic designer) started getting calls for contract work (not that he ever promoted himself in any way). He had been working at a large church and people loved how he was able to transform a white room into a beautiful atmosphere each weekend. Other churches, Christian events, and corporations started asking him to come design their spaces and create unique environments. One opportunity materialized after someone had seen his Instagram account, and those two weeks of work resulted in a full-time job opportunity that we eventually relocated our family for.

Every month that year, we sat on the edge of our seats in awe as his side business exceeded what my income had been. Even though there were weeks and months when we fumbled with confidence that we would be able to pay our bills, God's faithfulness and provision never wavered.

Truthfully, when opportunities surfaced that were appealing or "too good to be true," I struggled. The hustle chant from the experts told me I "needed" to take advantage of these things to further my writing and speaking dreams. Some were easy to reject because we simply couldn't afford to do them, but that didn't mean I wasn't overcome with jealousy when others could do what I could not.

Even more difficult was saying no to the jobs that would have provided extra income but at the cost of throwing myself back into a place of doing "all the things" instead of focusing on the few that I knew God wanted me to do. I am thankful for my husband, who was always quick to ask whether I was being obedient to God or hustling for a paycheck. It is such a blessing to have a spouse who not only makes great leaps of faith next to me but remains a constant encourager in the midst of the difficult places. He was the one to remind me of God's promises when I found myself faltering in moments of fear.

If we are honest, most of us would probably admit that starting something is usually not the hardest part; it's continuing onward after the momentum has slowed and the adrenaline has stopped pumping. We begin well—with a clear picture from God of what it is He wants us to do: write a book, volunteer at church, quit a job, start a nonprofit, foster some kids, finish our degree from ten years ago—you can fill in the blank. We hear God's voice. We write down the instruction and take off running. We aren't distracted by what others are doing because we have a goal and are laser-focused on it. But then, over time, we lose passion for it. There isn't much recognition in serving at church. The book proposal sits because we got bogged down in research. We tire of the battles, the long hours, the monotony of being a stay-at-home mom. And one morning we realize we have lost sight of the goal. Continued obedience is a challenge, but it's where the greatest growth tends to occur.

Jesus Himself paints a beautiful picture of what our lives will look like if we remain obedient and connected to Him: "I am the vine, and you are the branches. If you stay joined to me, and I to you, you will produce plenty of fruit. But separated from me you won't be able to do anything."[131]

Obedience was not John's word choice for this passage, but imagine how difficult it is to remain "connected" if you are not submitted to the One who provides for and sustains you. What kind of life is it to be "close" to the Vine but not yielded to it? Jesus went on to say that such branches are

---

[131] John 15:5 ERV

"deadwood, gathered up and thrown on the bonfire."[132]

There has been much conversation in Christian circles in recent years about remaining connected or joined to Jesus, about "abiding" in Him. And my question is, Can such abiding occur if we aren't acutely aware of His voice and eager to obey even His most simple instructions?

I love that John gives us the image of "plenty of fruit." In my mind, these are branches that are drooping under the weight of sun-sweetened fruit. The crop is begging to be picked and consumed; it is fat from an abundance of nourishment. And this is the promise of what our lives will look like. Jesus doesn't promise us a life bursting with fulfilled destiny, but with much fruit.

A plethora of fruit is the result of staying connected to Jesus. It cannot happen without Him. Jesus said, "You cannot be fruitful unless you remain in me."[133] This means, when He asks us to do something, we do it. Whether or not that task is something we feel "called to," are excited about, or think we will excel at. We don't have to believe that we are the right people for the job—if He has asked us, we are! And when we remain connected to Him, the result of our obedience is fruit. It may not be what we think of regarding fruitfulness, because we don't tend to look at things the way God does.[134]

When His whispers go against what others see as wisdom, when His task for us is not culturally acceptable, financially responsible, or in alignment with what our family, friends, or leadership may deem an "appropriate"

---

[132] John 15:5 MSG

[133] John 15:4 NLT

[134] 1 Samuel 16:7

use of our time, talent, or money—we balk. And when, years later, God's request is the same, without any deviation, it's even more difficult to stay the course. The missionary who has seen little in the way of "converts" may be tempted to throw in the towel, even when there has been an abundance of "fruit." When the business has failed to grow the way the plan promised, but there have been personal breakthroughs along the way, it may still be hard to resist the peer pressure to close up shop. When we find ourselves knee-deep in diapers and carpools, meal preparation and laundry, and we feel like God's command for us to "love our family" is getting in the way of the "big things" we were born to do, that's when He's leaning in and whispering, *"Will you continue to obey anyway?"* He wants to know that we will remain connected to Him even if we aren't thrilled about what He has asked us to do. God's gentle voice questions, *"Will you abide with Me in the mundane, in the monotonous, in the challenging, in the scary?"* It's in these moments, when it's easier to walk away than to put our heads down and dig deeper, that our faith is tested and we see how much fruit we are actually producing.

— — —

We started out discussing the word *hustle*—that popular notion that preys on our hearts by touting achievement and encouraging results at any cost. We compared work ethic to workaholism. We saw how "hard work" is different from "workaholism," which comes at a cost. We read about God's institution of labor, which was not the same as the original work handed down to Adam. We concluded that "hard work" as God mandated it is good, but when we begin sacrificing other things (or people) to achieve success (in any area), we've moved into the realm of workaholism, or *hustle*.

Next, we dove into the word *obedience*. We dissected it in an effort to understand our struggle with it—knowing that it often ensures our safety and protection. We recognized obedience as an internal choice of surrender, unlike hustle, which is a choice motivated by external, worldly "rewards." Obedience is a decision we make long before we act; it is the motive of our hearts. We obey out of a place of humility, yielding our will to something or someone else.

When I first started using the phrase "obedience over hustle," people seemed curious—but also confused. They weren't sure whether to fist-bump me, assuming that I was pro-hustle, or condemn me for being lazy or not serious enough about my craft or my influence (neither were true).

We tend to emphasize the idea of obedience in those matters we think God is most concerned with. Whom should we marry? Should we take the job offer, buy the house, forgive a spouse? We are quick to ask Him about serving on the worship team or hosting a small group, and we come to Him when we are faced with difficult situations, but if the matter is financial, we consult Dave Ramsey (no offense, Dave). If we want business advice, we open our Amazon app and download the latest *New York Times* bestseller to our Kindle. If our children are driving us bananas, we call our best friend, mother, or mentor, and if our marriage is faltering, we go searching for a three-day retreat that comes with a money-back guarantee. While none of these are bad options, they tend to be our first course of action. God's desire, however, is that He would be our first line of defense, not a last-ditch effort. We know His wisdom is greater than ours, as is His vantage point, but we live as though we can do better on our own. God wants to be a part of every area of our lives, not just invited into conversations when we have exhausted all other options.

For the rest of my life, the picture of a clenched fist will always be associated with the word *obey*. God whispering to me in the ballroom of that Indianapolis hotel was one of the most pivotal moments of my life. The way He gently told me, "*Malinda, trust Me. Open your hand. Surrender. Obey.*"

PART TWO:

Reflection and Small Group Questions

Chapter 10: What Happened to Obedience?

Have you ever gone to God with excuses only to feel that His response was, *"What does that matter?"*

What does obedience look like to you? How about as a spouse, a child, a parent, an employee?

Is "submission" more or less difficult for you to consider than "obedience"?

Do you think about your obedience as a part of your faith (or as a daily decision)? Why or why not?

Have you ever completed the easy part of a task, or the part you liked the most, and left the rest of the command alone (even though it came from God)?

Read Deuteronomy 11:26–28. What do you think this looks like for you today?

Read John 14:15. What does keeping God's commands look like on a daily basis?

When it comes to obeying God's commands, do some tend to trip you up more than others?

Consider/discuss this thought: *Obedience is both a choice and an act of faith. It doesn't require that we have all the answers or that we understand or even agree with the action requested.*

CHAPTER 11: JESUS: OBEDIENCE IN THE FLESH

Read Luke 22:39–46 and Hebrews 5:7–9.

Think about/discuss what it looked like for Jesus to be "obedient to death."

Read Matthew 26:36–46. Have you ever stopped to consider that Jesus chose obedience to His Father?

Does this fact make obedience easier or more difficult for you?

Read Luke 8:40–56. Have you ever thought about Jesus' delay in going to Jairus's daughter as obedience to His Father?

Does Jesus' delay in this story make you feel better about any situation you've recently entrusted to Him? Why or why not?

Read John 11:1–43 and consider how you would have felt if you were Mary or Martha.

Have there been moments when you've had doubts that God would intervene in time?

Consider/discuss this question: *What would happen if, when we came to God with our list of requests, we simply opened our hands and prayed like Jesus did: "Not my will, but Yours be done"?*

CHAPTER 12: COMPLETE OBEDIENCE

Describe a time when you saw God at work in the smallest details.

Consider/discuss this quote: *"The man's obedience activated the miracle."*

Read John 9:6–11. Have you ever stopped to think that obedience and healing are connected?

How do you feel about God's decision to strip King Saul of his throne in 1 Samuel 15:17–28?

Does this story change the way you view obedience to God's instructions? Why or why not?

Have you been guilty of completing only a part of what God asked you to do because you didn't like the request or thought that your way was better?

Read Numbers 20:8–12 and Proverbs 3:5–6. Can you think of a time when you trusted your own wisdom and it turned out better than God's plan?

Where do you need to obey completely? (For example, mending a relationship, setting priorities, overcoming an addiction, managing stress or anger, ordering your finances, or preparing for your future.)

Chapter 13: Obedient When the Dream Isn't Yours

How would things have turned out differently if Noah had disobeyed? *(Consider, for example, if he agreed to build the ark but didn't construct it to the exact specifications, gather every animal, or ensure an adequate food supply.)*

Consider/discuss this thought: *Obedience saved Noah.*
> Do you agree? Why or why not?

Has God ever laid out a very detailed plan for you?
> Did you follow it? What was the result?

Has God ever come to you with a plan that seemed ark-sized?
> If so, how did the plan make you feel?
> Did you argue with Him, listing all the reasons it was a crazy idea and asserting how unqualified you were?

Read Genesis 7:5. Can this be said of you?

Read Isaiah 55:8–11 and 1 Corinthians 1:25. Where are you guilty of assuming that you are smarter than God?

Chapter 14: Attitude Is Everything

Consider/discuss this question: *Many of us want God to ask us to do the "hard and heroic" things, the "great" things, and the "difficult" things; but when God responds with simple instructions, we storm off in a huff—just like Naaman.*

Read the story in 2 Kings 5:1–19. How do you feel after reading about God's simple instructions?

Have you ever been surprised (or felt free) when His response to your request was simple instead of complex or challenging?

Have you ever walked away in frustration or felt angry with God (or His messenger) because you didn't hear what you wanted?

Do you have people in your life, like Naaman did, who can speak truth to you? What are you doing to foster relationships with these individuals?

Read Proverbs 14:12 and 1 Corinthians 1:26–29.

Are you asking God for "great" or "difficult" tasks but scoffing at the small and simple things?

How often do we miss out on what God is doing because our attitudes need an adjustment?

Chapter 15: Obedience Equals Maturity

In what ways have you seen your faith grow? What is a task or decision you can look back on, knowing you once needed great faith or courage to carry it out, but today you could accomplish it easily?

Would you describe your relationship with Jesus (your faith journey) as one that is "moving along," or has it become more stationary?

Read James 2:14–26. How are you flexing your faith muscles?

Where can you take steps to give more financially and relationally (for example, opening your home; sharing your gifts, your time, your resources)?

Where is God calling you to grow bolder in your faith—sharing the good news with family members, friends, co-workers, neighbors?

Read Genesis 22:15–18 and Matthew 5:16. What do these verses say about our faith and our works being connected?

Can our faith mature without obedience?

Consider/discuss this quote: *"It is obedience that moves us from one point in our faith to the next—not a mere feeling or a belief. Obedience is active participation, not just a nod of acknowledgment. It is continuous; it is the progression of our faith from fragile and helpless to courageous and tenacious.*

Obedience is choosing to let God lead and falling in behind Him with humility, not passivity. Obedience is faith in action, and the result is a maturity that can come only as we move in the direction He's asked—repeatedly."

CHAPTER 16: OBEDIENCE WHEN THE PATH IS UNCLEAR

Have you ever felt like Danielle from the beginning of the chapter—longing for an answer from God, unsure of what to do next?

What is the last thing God asked you to do?

If you can't remember, answer this question honestly: Have you lost sight of your first love, Jesus (see Revelation 2:4)?

How much time are you spending with God (in prayer and in the Word)?

Have you ever been afraid of messing up God's plan for your life, of walking outside His will, of missing something if you didn't move quickly enough?

What happened when you finally did make a decision and move?

Read Luke 1:1–4 and consider the last "good idea" you had. Did you do it?

Have you ever stepped into a decision completely sure that

it was God's will, only to realize quickly that the decision wasn't so great or even healthy?

How did you feel when you had to stop and turn around?

Consider/discuss this idea: *"It's a lot harder to fall out of the will of God than you think."*

Chapter 17: Obedience: Not Just Direction but Pace

Think about the quote from the beginning of the chapter: *"The right thing, at the wrong time, is the wrong thing."*

Do you agree? Has there been a time in your life when you pursued the right thing at the wrong time?

Read Jeremiah 29:11. Have you claimed this verse yet failed to ask God about His best timing?

Have you ever been thankful that God didn't answer your prayer (or give you your heart's desire) in the timing you wanted?

What happened instead?

Where has your hustle brought hurt or disaster as in the case of Abraham, Sarah, and Hagar?

Delay does not mean denial. Describe how this thought makes you feel.

Consider/discuss this quote: *"God didn't waste a single moment in either Joseph or David's life. Everything they endured, every lesson, each opportunity, was part of a greater plan. At times we need to remember that God's plan for our life is the greater plan—it's not the end He cares about so much as what's happening inside of us along the way."*

CHAPTER 18: EXCHANGING FEAR FOR OBEDIENCE

Read Judges 6:12–16. What did God say after Gideon gave his list of excuses?

Have you ever sung the Gideon song to God? *"I'm too small, uneducated, poor, unqualified."* What was God's response?

What is your go-to excuse for not doing what God (or someone else) has asked you to do?

How would you respond if God asked you to cut all but one-tenth of your support on the eve of some gigantic project you'd been preparing for?

Have you been guilty of looking for confirmation from others instead of trusting God at His word?
    Where do you need to move from fear to obedience?

What words has God spoken over you?
    Have you accepted and acted on them, or, like Gideon, are you still hiding from them?

Where have you allowed insecurity, fear, or doubt to trump what God has called you to do?

Consider/discuss this question: *If God calls you "brave warrior," regardless of your circumstances, who are you to say otherwise?*

Meditate on these additional scriptures: Psalm 34:4; Isaiah 41:10; John 14:27.

CHAPTER 19: COURAGEOUS OBEDIENCE

Have you ever told God how the miracle needs to be performed?

Did you ever expect Him to move in your life in the same way twice?

Read Joshua 1. What does the word *brave* mean to you?

How does the phrase "courageous obedience in the midst of fear" make you feel?

Describe a time when what God was asking you to do required courageous obedience.

Read Deuteronomy 31:7–8, 23. Moses repeatedly told the people and Joshua not to be afraid. God spoke these words over Joshua also. They needed to be reminded continually.

Have you ever considered that your obedience could be

the encouragement that others need to step out in faith for themselves?

Consider/discuss the following thought: *The journey probably looks different, as do the specific directions God gives each of us to obey, but what others catch as they watch you step out into your river is the message, "If she can do it, then so can I." Your courage empowers others to move in the direction God is leading them.*

What flooded river has God asked you to step into? Have you moved from the shore to the water? If so, what happened?

CHAPTER 20: FRUITFUL OBEDIENCE

Do you have a problem with starting what God has asked you to do? Or is it more difficult for you to continue once the momentum has slowed?

Read John 15:4–6. Are you producing "much fruit" (v. 5 NIV)? A little fruit? Some fruit?

Are you connected to the Vine?
    What does that look like for you?
    How do you know when you are no longer connected?

How does the fruitfulness of your life connect to your obedience—to the extent to which you abide in Jesus?

Have you sequestered obedience to God in a box titled "spiritual" but kept God out of other parts of your life, such as your finances, marriage, or career?

Consider/discuss this quote: *"Continued obedience is a challenge, but it's where the greatest growth tends to occur."*

Where is God asking you to open your hand, to surrender, to obey Him fully?

CONCLUSION

Continued Obedience

I feel like God is asking me to jump," he confided with conviction.

It was Sunday afternoon, and our family was making the trek home from church. The sun was shining, it was a warm Fall day in northern California, and my heart was full. The service had been precisely what we needed—balm to our spirits after a particularly difficult week. We had chatted with friends and, more importantly, connected with God through songs, prayers, and moments of quiet that enveloped our hurts and questions with grace and peace.

Our kids were running down the street toward our house (and lunch), having turned the corner into the safety zone of our neighborhood where they were allowed to venture a little farther away from Mom and Dad. My husband was holding my hand as we strolled at a more leisurely pace than our children, and when I glanced up at his face, I couldn't contain my smirk.

"You know what this week is, don't you?" I began. Without waiting for him to respond (which is fairly typical for me), I continued, "It was three years ago this week that I quit my job." The words couldn't escape my mouth without also pulling my eyebrows upward—my entire face asking the question: "Coincidence?"

We don't believe in coincidences, having noted too

many times the precision with which God moves in our lives; unexpected bills that arrive with totals equal to the checks we pull from the mailbox; timelines that seem to be stitched together regarding new homes being purchased or old ones sold; and jobs that fall into our laps with impeccable timing. We've accepted the fact that God is always moving in our lives and have stopped to acknowledge the way in which He does—always with order and intention, never tardily or in a haphazard way.

That afternoon, after the kids had eaten lunch and found something quiet to entertain themselves with for a couple of hours, we circled back to our earlier conversation. "What are the odds that I would be editing my manuscript, needing to finish the conclusion, during the very same time that you are about to launch your own business?" I couldn't help but chuckle at the irony that this whole message of choosing obedience over hustle started when God asked me to surrender my job—to relinquish control regarding our finances, to obey what He was asking me to do, to trust Him to be our provider. And now, three years later, my husband was gearing up to take a similar (though exponentially riskier) step.

A few days later, after unsuccessfully trying to go back to sleep, I shuffled out to the kitchen to make myself some tea and settled on the couch with my Bible and journal. I knew in my heart the decision that we were about to make—God had made it so incredibly clear that past Sunday—but my mind was having a hard time catching up with my heart. For days I had landed on one side of the decision or the other, flip-flopping between courage and excitement, doubt and fear. I knew I needed time with the Lord, without the music of the worship team playing in the background or the voice of a teacher sharing one-liners, whether from scripture or not.

About an hour had passed when I heard the unmistakable scuffing of my husband's slippered feet coming down the hallway. His sleep had been peaceful, evident in the way he yawned and snuggled into the space next to me. His smile told me both "good morning" and that he knew I had something to tell him. When I told him I agreed with his statement about feeling like it was time for him to jump, it was with teary eyes and a crackly voice. I shared the mental image that I'd had many times prior—he knows it well—of being perched on the side of a mountain, with the base-jumping suit all ready to catch the wind. "Except this time," I whispered, "I wasn't standing alone." I choked on the words as I whispered, "You were holding my hand, and Jesus was holding your hand—and we were all about to jump together, babe."

I knew well the terror of turning my back on what made sense, on what was easy and acceptable, for the wild adventure of saying yes to God. Yes, jumping with God is exhilarating. Yes, you're in the company of great men and women of faith. Yes, it is a beautiful story to share with the greatest victories to celebrate. But before you can jump, you have to stare fear in the face. You have to stand perched on the edge of a cliff, feeling both the unforgiving sun and the bristle of the wind. You have to go through the motions of "suiting up" and preparing your body for the free fall.

Fortunately, one of us had already stood in that place, holding both the terror and anticipation simultaneously. One of us had already said yes to obeying God's leading and had experienced the peace that comes when the heart has surrendered. What was on the other side of the jump was total dependence on God, our wills completely yielded to His plan and His timeline.

--- --- ---

Surrendering to God can feel like an effortless decision if it means that we get to jump at a great opportunity or pursue something we are already passionate about. If we are able to use the skills and abilities He has placed inside of us (those we naturally excel at), then we tend to be more compliant. Then there are the moments when God comes to us with big asks that, though not a part of our five-year plan, we quickly get on board with because it's a good cause, a fun adventure, or something that will make us feel good about our obedience. At times, it's easy for us to step up willingly and obey promptly:

God, You want me to go on a mission trip? You've got it! I've always wanted to go to Uganda!

Lord, You want us to adopt a baby? Okay, we never felt settled about the size of our family.

Father, You want me to lead a small group? I love hanging out with teenagers.

This type of obedience requires little risk and tends to come with loads of gratification. We love knowing that our lives are making a difference, and the recognition and validation are great motivators to obey God when He comes calling. It feels good to be needed, and we like to shine, especially when we are using our "God-given gift" to bless others. But what do we do when His ask is out of our comfort zone?

Truthfully, the more difficult decisions come when we are asked to do something in obscurity or when we are required to put our money where our mouths are.

How well do we obey when no one is watching? How do we feel about God's command to serve in anonymity? How quick are we to move when God asks us to jump with Him off a cliff, without any idea what the future holds? Are we equally as excited to submit to His timeline when He asks us to wait instead of providing the perfect job, or when He tells us to fix our finances before having a baby, or when He suggests that we need to focus on being a good neighbor, or when He asks us to quit our job and stay home with our kids?

Serve in student ministry? Lord, we just got our last child out the door to college! This is supposed to be "my season" to do what I want!

Foster a child? You can't be serious, God. We both work full-time and are paying off school loans.

Live on less and support a full-time missionary? Wouldn't it be better if I took my youth group on a mission trip instead?

Sometimes what God asks us to do is what we want, but often it will require more from us than what we want to give and typically for longer than we expect. That is what continued obedience looks like. It is carefully tending to what He has commissioned us to do, sometimes without being able to see the light at the end of the tunnel. It's not just a onetime risk or a single act, but faithfully putting our hand to what God has led us to do.

He may be calling you to be the best mother you can be to your children without comparing yourself to everyone else, to love the elderly couple next door who don't have any family in the area, or to be a light in your work-place, where you are surrounded by individuals who oppose your values and beliefs—all without any promise of those watered seeds bearing fruit. When God asks us to love the spouse who hurt us, extend our arms to the prodigal son or daughter, forgive the friend who betrayed us—these are the times we may struggle to continue the way He is leading.

— — —

Obedience equals movement; it is the opposite of idle or apathetic living. It means uncurling our hands and opening our hearts. Obedience is not just a good idea or a feeling we can dismiss when we aren't in the mood. Obedience is a heart issue, and that's what God is always after—hearts that are wholly surrendered and devoted to Him.

Obedience means being completely compliant rather than omitting what we don't like and filling in the blanks without consulting Him.

Obedience is movement from a posture of humility and submission because we understand that God's plans are better. It is choosing His way over our own. It's laying down what we think best—our timing and our methods—and yielding to what God thinks is best. It's making the consistent and conscious decision to listen for His voice in all matters, not just in the areas where we think He'll have an opinion. It's living with the knowledge that His opinion is the only one that matters and that seeking Him first is a command worth following. When we live like this, we are choosing obedience over hustle.

Obedience over Hustle Manifesto

I choose to yield to God's pace,
  even when Hustle barks, "Go faster!"
I choose to stay in my lane, paying no heed as
  Hustle dispenses a distracting double portion
  of comparison.
I choose to believe that God's vantage point is
  better, even as Hustle taunts, "This is the
  only way."
I choose to serve others rather than clawing
  my way into the spotlight, as Hustle
  implies I should do.
I choose the wisdom of building slow, while
  Hustle smirks at small and anonymous
  offerings.
I choose to walk patiently rather than sprinting
  toward a goal because Hustle demands,
  "Do it now."
I choose rest, knowing it is for the strong
  not the weak, as Hustle accuses.
I choose to be a kingdom builder, even though
  Hustle endorses growing my personal empire.
I choose to train my ear to hear God's voice,
  while Hustle dictates that I listen to the masses.
I choose to pursue only a few things instead
  of adhering to Hustle's expectation
  that I do all the things.
I choose obedience to God—to His timing and
  His way—over the need to be affirmed
  by Hustle.
I choose *Obedience over Hustle.*

ACKNOWLEDGMENTS

Alex, you believe in my dreams as if they are your own, and probably more than I do at times. You walk your own path of obedience with more grace and integrity than anyone I know. We are better together, and I am so thankful for this incredible adventure that we're on.

Lydia and Madelyn, my wolf-pack pups, I am so thankful for the amazing cheerleaders that you've been throughout this process. You are my treasures, and I pray that you always have the courage to say yes to Jesus—no matter what He asks of you.

Tabitha, I have run this race well because you stayed next to me with every step. You fleshed out more of these ideas than anyone else and have watched the book evolve from a phone conversation into something so much bigger than we ever could have thought. I am grateful that you have carried this message as if it were your own. Let's celebrate!

Bekah, thank you for holding my hand through this past year, for assuring me, asking questions, and listening. You have a gift, and I'm so glad that you make time for people. Can't wait to sit on your porch one day.

To the many (writing) friends who have rallied behind me: Sarah, Lindsay, Rachel, Beth, Jennifer, Michelle, and others, I am deeply grateful for your listening ears. You haven't tired of this message but continued to hold up my hands. I am so thankful to have you in my corner.

To the team of editors who read the many versions of these pages along the way, who pushed me to tell the story better, and forced me out of my comfort zone, I am forever in your debt. You are heroes.

To the team at Barbour Publishing, Sharon Farnell, and Jim Hart, thank you for taking a chance on a new author with a lot of passion, but little platform. You have made a way for this dream to come to fruition, and I couldn't be more grateful for your, *Yes.*

To the readers who hold these words, thank you for diving into these pages. I pray that your faith is stirred and your heart encouraged. May you hear the whispers of God when He calls you to trust Him, to surrender, and to obey, and may you have the courage to live your life choosing *obedience over hustle.*

About the Author

Malinda Fuller is a bold communicator who is passionate about thriving couples and families and helping people grow as disciples of Jesus. Malinda and her husband, Alex, have been married for over fourteen years and have served on staff at several churches and ministries for even longer. Their love for travel has taken them to nearly every state and across Canada—Malinda's home and native land. She is a proud homeschooling mom to two spirited girls, and their self-dubbed "wolf pack" family is always up for an adventure.

Malinda's writing has been featured in multiple publications, and she offers regular #obedienceoverhustle encouragement to her newsletter subscribers at malindafuller.com and on Instagram as @malinda.fuller.